CLIMBING YOUR SELF-DISCIPLINE TREE

THE THREE STAGES ESSENTIAL FOR ACCOMPLISHING ANY GOAL

ZACH MATHEWS

Copyright © 2021 Zach Mathews

First published 2021 by Zach Mathews Writing

The rights of Zach Mathews to be identified as the author of this work has been asserted to him in accordance with the Copyright Act of 1976.

All rights reserved. No part of this publication may be reproduced, stored in a retrieval system, or transmitted in any other form or by any means, electronic, mechanical, photocopying, recording or otherwise, without the prior permission of the publisher.

ISBN: 978-1-7377415-1-0

www.zachmathewswriting.com

*To my beautiful wife, Bre.
You are my rock, my inspiration, and my best friend.
You've always encouraged me to chase my dreams;
Now, thanks to you, it's become a reality.
I love you.*

Contents

INTRODUCTION	7
PHASE 1: PREPARATION	15
CHAPTER 1 Vision	17
CHAPTER 2 Goal-Setting	41
CHAPTER 3 Organization	65
CHAPTER 4 Cleansing	85
PHASE 2: PRODUCTION	107
CHAPTER 5 Exercise	109
CHAPTER 6 Nutrition	125
CHAPTER 7 Well-Being	143
CHAPTER 8 Execution	169

PHASE 3: PERSISTENCE	**183**
CHAPTER 9 Perseverance	**185**
CHAPTER 10 Reputation	**199**
CHAPTER 11 Accountability	**215**
CONCLUSION	**235**
ACKNOWLEDGMENTS	**243**
NOTES	**247**

INTRODUCTION

How in the world am I going to pull this off? That's what I thought to myself as I prepared to apply for jobs during my last semester of college in the fall of 2015. I remember it all too well.

Over the summer, I'd gotten engaged to my dream girl. Even though we walked graduation together that May, I still had *one* more semester left before I officially graduated. So while she was about to start a full-time position at the infamous Water Tower Place in Downtown Chicago, I was back in Angola, Indiana taking online quizzes.

That's when it hit me: I'm supposed to be starting my *career* in less than *four months*. You know, that thing I'd been working towards the past four years.

By the time the semester was done in December, I was expected to have a job lined up in professional sports (I majored in Sports Management). The only problem was that I had zero connections inside the professional sports industry and zero relevant experience to the job I would be applying for. When the employer took a look at my resume, it wouldn't exactly scream, *"Hi! I'm the next Zig Ziglar of professional sports sales!"*

So what was I prepared to do to make that happen?

I remember hopping on one of the computers in my college's library and researching how to get a job in sports. During my research, I came across a website that saved my life. It was (and still is) a site where all professional sports teams post all of the positions they're actively looking to fill.

I made myself a promise that day: I would visit that site every day and apply to every entry-level position I could find; it didn't matter what league the team was in or where the team was located—all I wanted was a chance.

I kept that promise to myself.

I logged on every day (often two to three times) and applied for every entry-level position. By the time December rolled around, I had applied to more than 200 different positions on that one website alone. I went on 30 first round interviews, 12 second-round interviews, and made it to the final stages of the interview process with three separate teams. As a matter of fact, I had *two* job offers on the table during the week of final exams.

Had it not been for what I call **successful self-discipline**, I wouldn't have landed a job in the sports industry. The two positions I eventually got offers from were both posted on a Friday night. It would've been just as easy for me to say, *"I've worked hard all week, I'm going to get an early start on the weekend."* Instead, I kept doing small things to increase my chances of *eventually* finding a job. I ended up taking a sales position with the Arizona Coyotes in Glendale, Arizona, which is where my career began.

That's the thing about self-discipline, folks: it's all about your **commitment to the details**. If you're willing to stick it out and have a mindset of *"this* will *work!"* then there's *nothing* you can't accomplish.

Before you read this book, I want you to know that successful self-discipline doesn't have one distinct model—it's different for everyone. This book isn't meant to fix you, because you aren't broken; rather, it's meant to give you a head start by clarifying what constructive self-discipline looks like. From there, you can use the content in this book to look yourself in the mirror, see what you do well, realize what needs work and discover a few ideas on how to implement change.

Self-discipline isn't about being a strict auditor of your everyday life, either; it's about creating healthy steps towards achieving your goals in your faith, your family, your career and your personal lives.

It's my personal opinion that most people lack healthy self-discipline; we work for the weekends, not for our calling. Instead of prioritizing meditation and learning, we pick up our phones and scroll. That's not to say that you should incinerate your smartphone and never use it again; I'm merely suggesting that there's a balance to be had. You should prioritize your personal and professional growth over what your friends are posting on their Instagram stories. Instead of picking up your phone, pick up a new hobby!

Before you read on, I want you to accept control of your self-discipline. *Successful* self-discipline always begins by accepting the fact that you (yes, *you!*) control your path to success. While there are certainly factors outside of your control, you can't fixate on them. It all starts by envisioning the proper path for achieving your goals and understanding how self-discipline plays a role in that journey.

CLIMBING YOUR SELF-DISCIPLINE TREE

When I was a kid, I used to *love* climbing trees. I was a hyperactive child, so my parents would send me outside to play on a tree that was located in the common ground next to our house. From what I can remember, it was a Bradford Pear tree, which meant the branches were low enough for kids to reach them from the ground. I spent many hours climbing that tree with my little sister, and other kids that lived near us.

Climbing Your Self-Discipline Tree

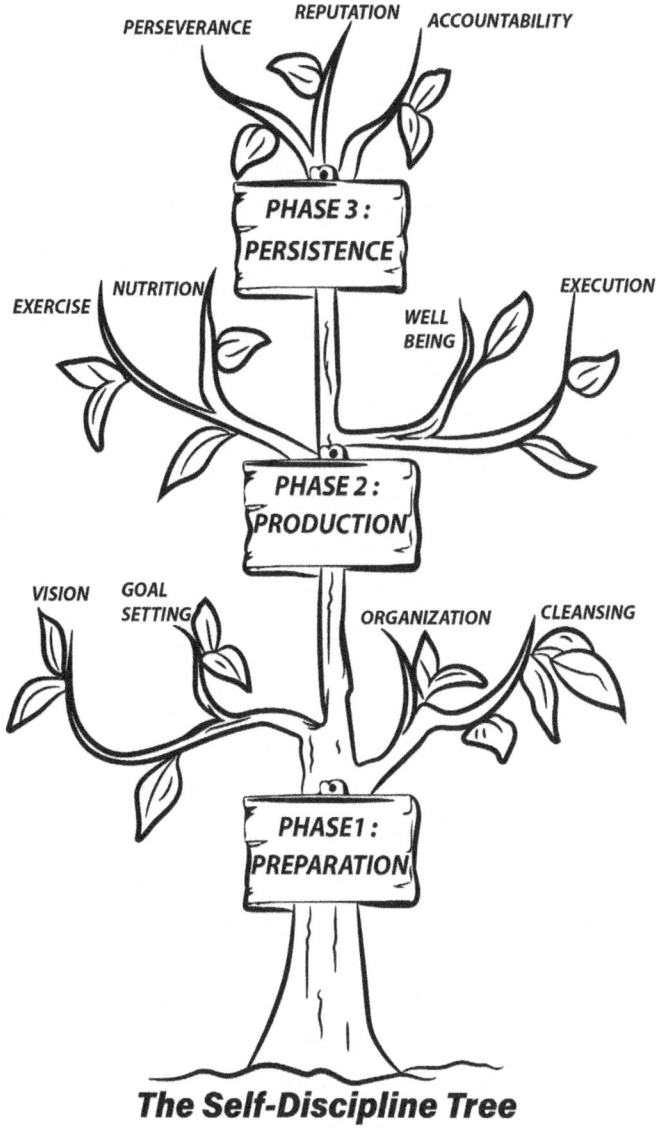

The Self-Discipline Tree

Whenever we'd go to the tree, I had one goal: to climb to the top. I always made sure I had enough time to make it up to the top (and back down again) before my parents would call me home. I can't tell you how many times I got stuck, scared or injured in some way; but no matter what happened the day before, me and all the other kids were back at that tree the very next day, with the goal of reaching the top once again!

This is a perfect representation of what self-discipline should look like in our daily lives. If the tree represents the goal you have for yourself, then the very top of that tree should represent the moment when you've accomplished that goal.

There's only two things you need to do: First, identify the tree (the goal) you want to climb. Second, start climbing by pulling yourself up on the lowest branch.

Before you even start the climb though, know that there will be setbacks ahead. But here's a question for you: when you experience a setback while climbing the tree, are you the type of person to look up and see how *close* you are to the top, or look down and see how *far* you are from the bottom? Your answer says a lot about how you currently view your self-discipline.

If you consistently look down, you might quickly become uncomfortable—even scared—of how far you are from the safety and security of the ground below. However, if you constantly look up, you'll increase your chances of reaching the top successfully by viewing the positive and reaching for the next closest branch.

In this book, we will uncover three key phases to help you integrate successful self-discipline into your life and reach the top of any tree (goal) you've set your eyes on. In order to help you understand this concept, I've created a teaching tool that I like to call the "Self-Discipline Tree" (drumroll, please!).

Think about any cartoon Evergreen tree you've ever seen. Typically, these drawings show a tree with a sturdy trunk, pointy top and are separated by three distinct groups of branches. In our Self-Discipline Tree illustration, those three groups of branches represent the three separate phases of successful self-discipline: Preparation, Production and Persistence. We'll illustrate these phases on the tree going from the bottom to the top—just like how you'd climb a tree.

Phase One —the Preparation Phase—is all about setting your goals up for success. This initial step towards achieving your goals is when you pull yourself up over the lowest branch. Each chapter in this phase—Vision, Goal-Setting, Organization and Cleansing—will guide you through how to envision the road ahead and cut out as many potential setbacks as possible, as well as prepare for the obstacles ahead.

In Phase Two—the Production Phase—we'll uncover what aspects are important to implement as you start to take action and aggressively climb your tree. The chapters in Phase Two—Exercise, Nutrition, Well-Being and Execution—are all about establishing healthy habits that will make your journey more manageable. These aspects of production can help you maintain self-discipline in every phase of your life and, more importantly, have *fun* while you reach for your goals.

Lastly, in Phase Three—the Persistence Phase—we will unwrap the key factors that are essential to overcoming failure when (not *if*) it occurs. Everyone fails, but you can easily handle those setbacks by approaching the process the right way. Each chapter of Phase Three—Perseverance, Reputation and Accountability—are aimed at giving you direction. You'll learn about the strength of a support system, how your personal brand plays a role and what true perseverance entails.

As I stated before, my goal isn't to *fix* you, it's to *help* you. I've filled this book with stories, tools and exercises—like my "Bing-Goal Board" goal organization tool—to help make your goals feel credible, and help you remember to *have fun* along the way. My hope is that you'll find these resources helpful in igniting the self-discipline you've had inside you all along.

Without further ado, let's start climbing your tree!

PHASE 1:

PREPARATION

Chapter 1

VISION

Back in my senior year of high school, I was a complete mess; I had no sense of direction, no concept of my future, no interest in my school work... nothing. All I wanted to do was play lacrosse and be the class clown. Believe it or not, despite my lack of interest in my grades, I *actually* thought I was going to play college lacrosse somewhere. Surely grades were just a formality, right?

Throughout my senior season, college coaches would chat with me at my winter league games and email me to schedule campus tours. However, at one point or another, they'd all say the same thing: have your school counselor send me your cumulative grade point average (GPA) and coursework.

Unsurprisingly, their interest in me attending their college would fade shortly after that; no coach wanted to touch my transcripts with a 10-foot pole. Even if they *wanted* to, their university would never accept me. I remember walking across the stage at graduation wondering, *"So what do I do now?"*

Looking back, my problem wasn't that I was lazy or too stupid to complete my coursework; I lacked *vision*.

I had absolutely *no* concept of what lied ahead of me once I was handed my high school diploma on stage. Life had to smack me in the face and tell me, *"You aren't playing college lacrosse,"* before I realized my own lack of perception ruined my dream.

Once I finally woke up to this harsh reality, I did the only thing I could think of—I enrolled at my local community college. I remember being so pissed off at the world, when really, all I had was myself to blame.

Two years later, I couldn't take it anymore. I was tired of seeing my former high school teammates play college lacrosse while I attended community college part-time and sold shoes at Dick's Sporting Goods. My grades were better, my passion to play was still there—I was *determined* to play college lacrosse somewhere the following school year.

To make it a reality, I reached out to my high school coach and *begged* him to let me be an assistant coach that spring season (to my surprise, he agreed!). So every day that spring was spent coaching lacrosse, going to my classes, working part-time, working out and emailing as many college coaches as I could.

Within a short amount of time, not only did I find an interested coach, I had *three* different colleges interested in me. I eventually chose to play at Trine University, where I became Senior Captain and—more importantly—met my future wife!

I'm not telling you this story to brag about my college lacrosse days. Truth be told, there wasn't much to brag about from a statistical standpoint; I certainly wasn't piling up goals or assists. My role on the team was playing short stick defensive midfielder—a position given to midfielders who can't score.

Instead, I tell you this story because it shows the role that vision plays in your self-discipline. Without vision, I was completely lost. My laziness and disinterest in high school had nothing to do with being 18 years old; it was due to a lack of vision. I never took the time to envision a future and, as a result, I had nothing to work towards. In my mind, I had no reason to care about school, no reason to study for tests or pay attention in class.

As soon as I could envision the path towards my goal (playing lacrosse in college), I worked tirelessly to achieve it. I finally took the time to look inward and acknowledge what made me special as a person, then used it to create an opportunity for myself.

Self-discipline starts with vision, and vision starts with finding your gift. Let's start there!

I. Finding Your Gift

Sadly, some people go their entire lives without finding their gift; they—sometimes unknowingly—settle for the mediocre and the comfortable. Rather than climbing the tree, they choose to stand on the ground their whole life and stare at the top—at what *could* be.

Think about that for a moment.

The truth is, you have something to offer this world that *no one* else can. God created you at this very moment for a distinct purpose; you owe it to yourself and to others to figure out what that is.

To quote the legendary artist, Pablo Picasso, "The meaning of life is to find your gift. The purpose of life is to give it away."[1]

When doing my research for this book, I thought it would be cool to send a survey out to some of the most influential businessmen and businesswomen that I've come across to see how their careers began, and to understand the role that self-discipline played in their career.

One of those people was Steve Gonzales, the Vice President of Group Memberships and Events for the Arizona Coyotes. He shared how he got his start as an intern for a Minor League Baseball team. (For those of you that don't know, interns and employees of Minor League teams have to do a little bit of everything, and I mean *everything;* they're instructed to sell tickets during the day, roll out the tarp during rain delays, put on the smelly mascot uniform… you name it!)

Despite wearing many different hats throughout each day, Steve called his time as an intern a "humbling experience." Not only did it give him a foot in the door, it was where he found his internal gifts: building relationships and serving the community.

I can attest that both of these gifts serve him well in his current role with the Coyotes. In my time with the franchise, Steve was always willing to provide me (and other ticket sales representatives) with direction.

The moral of Steve's story is this: your personal gifts are found through *action*. In order to find what makes you special, you have to get out there and *experience* things.

As a matter of fact, you won't likely find your gifts until you undergo a bit of adversity or struggle. Steve found his while working at a Minor League Baseball team without pay. While balancing ten job duties at any given moment, he was able to prioritize what gift was non-negotiable to him: serving others.

On the contrary, it took me several years to realize that serving people and selling tickets wasn't *my* thing. I gave it everything I had, but eventually my lack of self-fulfillment in the position left me frustrated and burnt out. It was at that point that I discovered what my *true* gift was: writing.

Looking back at my life, that truth was right in front of me all along. When I was in fifth grade, I distinctly remember writing stories, drawing pictures for those stories and bringing them into school the next day to show my teacher. When my buddies and I had a podcast, we launched a website and I *volunteered* to write articles for it.

However, it didn't click for me that that was my gift until I took action under adversity. I realized my current career wasn't for me and I needed a change; that's when I landed a side hustle job as a Content Writer. Eventually, I turned that into my full-time gig and the rest is history!

Staying AWAKE

So how can you take action to find your gift? Where do you start? That part, my friend, is completely up to *you*. My advice is to get involved in an activity you're interested in; if you're passionate about dogs, volunteer at a shelter; if you love baseball, find a travel baseball team or high school team for which you can become an assistant coach. Everyone has to start *somewhere*!

Once you get involved in your passion, you'll be amazed at how quickly your gifts reveal themselves; all you have to do is keep the right perspective throughout. But what does that look like?

Many people have asked me what it took to find my gift. How can you stay perceptive while also trying to accomplish a task? For example, if you become an assistant baseball coach for a high school team, how can you keep an open mind to notice when your gifts show their beautiful faces?

My advice is to stay AWAKE.

No, I'm not advocating that you deprive yourself of sleep; it's an acronym that I created to help describe the right mindset for finding your gift. It encourages you to stay **A**ware, **W**illing, **A**vailable, **K**nowledgeable and **E**nthusiastic. Let me break it down for you in more detail, word by word.

Stay Aware—In order to find your gift, you need to stay alert. What are you doing when you feel most alive? What parts of your job or life do you most look forward to? What activities do you enjoy doing no matter how much effort is involved? I guarantee you that your gift lies in those moments.

Stay Willing—Not knowing your own gift(s) can be frustrating, but let me ask you this: what if you've never found your gift because you've never *tried* it before? Always remain willing to try new things. When you find yourself kick-started by a new passion, your personal gift is close at hand!

Stay Available—Opportunity seems to occur at the most random of times; it's up to you to remain ready and available for when it comes knocking at your door. Remain available to lend a helping hand whenever anybody needs it; never say "no" to an opportunity to help—it could be the start of something new! You'll be surprised how brightly your talents shine through when you stray from your normal, everyday routine.

Stay Knowledgeable—If your personal gifts and talents show up when you feel most alive, then you need to keep feeding yourself those moments. Always stay knowledgeable of different careers and opportunities that allow you to do what you're most passionate about; research new positions, learn about how your biggest role models got their start and network with everyone you meet. Even if *you* don't realize your gifts, someone else might and they'll give you a chance to maximize them.

Stay Enthusiastic—This is often the hardest one. It can be defeating to constantly search for your gift and come up empty-handed. Trust me, I know. But you *have* to keep a positive and optimistic attitude, no matter how long it takes. Your gifts *will* shine through. Your destiny *will* unravel itself eventually; it's only a matter of time!

II. Inspiration and Motivation

Often times, inspiration and motivation are paired as one and the same. It may surprise you to learn that there is a *very* discernible difference between the two. While both can be defined as a force that's pulling you to do something, they come from two vastly different places.

Inspiration comes from *inside of you.* For one reason or another, your emotions and thoughts create a force inside of you that ignites a fire. Meanwhile, motivation is a force that comes from *an outside source* that drives you to take an action, whatever that might be.

Imagine that you are a car (weird, I know, but hear me out!). If you received inspiration, then you would find it easy to turn the ignition, push down on your accelerator and head out to your desired destination as quickly as possible. However, if you received motivation, then your internal engine wouldn't start. Instead, you'd be carried away by a tow truck in order to reach your final destination (at a much slower pace, I might add). So what role does inspiration and motivation play in successful self-discipline? If you want to climb your tree and reach the top, which one do you need? The answer is both; let's find out why!

Understanding Inspiration

If you take nothing else away from this book, please absorb this: successful self-discipline isn't about exerting maximum effort all of the time in every single thing you do. If *that's* what it was, then I certainly wouldn't be writing a book on the subject.

Rather, successful self-discipline is all about recognizing which aspects of your life (which goals) you *want* to exert maximum effort into. It's also about acknowledging what goals you don't need to exert as much energy into but can still get fulfillment out of.

I'll give you an example. I personally want to exert as much effort as I can into my faith, my family and my writing. Those three things are where my priorities lie; they surpass all else. Until the day I die, I'll put as much energy as I have into them.

While my fitness is an important piece of the puzzle for me, I'm not training to become a bodybuilder. I get my fulfillment from staying in shape, having confidence in my physique and actively avoiding the dreaded "dad bod" at all costs, but it's not everything to me.

It's all about finding the "why" behind your goals. *Why* do you want to get up at 5 a.m. to work out—to gain more self-confidence? *Why* do you dream of landing the VP position at your firm—because it helps you quantify your self-worth? Does that make you shallow? Of course not! It helps you to be honest with yourself so that you can exert the necessary effort to get your fulfillment out of that goal.

You might be wondering how this ties into inspiration. Well, where do you think your effort and energy *comes* from? It comes from the force that you summon inside yourself. Motivation alone can't push you to accomplish your goals. You won't become the CEO of a company from an outside force pulling you along. Your inspiration is what's needed to maximize your daily effort and work towards that lofty (yet entirely possible) goal.

Can I tell you what *my* biggest inspiration is? It's proving people wrong. I love getting the chance to silence my critics. It's a significant reason why I've written this book. In all my years of education (college included), I've only had *one* teacher/professor tell me I had a knack for writing; now it's what I do for a living. As much as I love proving her right, I get more enjoyment out of proving the other 15 of them wrong. Tell me that I *can't* do something and I'll prioritize my entire routine to make you eat those words.

What's *your* focal point of inspiration? If you aren't sure, think back to a few recent goals you've accomplished. Why were you able to stick to those goals and see them through? What pushed you to achieve them? If you assess them long enough and hard enough, you'll notice a pattern; that pattern is your main source of inspiration. Use it to your advantage!

Understanding Motivation

Did you know that there are two types of motivation? The motivation that you receive can be categorized as either intrinsic motivation or extrinsic motivation.

Intrinsic motivation is doing something because you find it personally rewarding. This is often confused with inspiration, but—in my opinion—there's a slight difference: Inspiration is more attached to feelings and emotions; motivation is more attached to personal satisfaction. I'll give you an example of it in a second.

Extrinsic motivation is when you perform an act because you want to either earn a reward or avoid a punishment for *not* doing something.[2]

The odds are highly likely that, growing up, you found yourself staring at a messy bedroom once or twice. If you had intrinsic motivation, you would clean your room because you got satisfaction out of having a clean and organized space. Meanwhile, with extrinsic motivation, you'd clean your room because your mom told you to. In that scenario, you wouldn't clean your room out of your personal interests; you'd clean it because you wanted to avoid getting grounded or you wanted to get an allowance for doing the job right.

Both types of motivation are essential to establishing successful self-discipline. As we'll discuss in the next section, you won't always have the strength to push yourself forward; there will be times when you falter. That's called "being *human*." It's in those moments when we need our loved ones to give us extrinsic motivation to keep pushing. If you're going to reach the top of your tree, you sometimes need someone at the bottom saying "If you reach the top, I'll buy you an ice cream cone!" Go ahead... Tell me that wouldn't make climbing the tree easier.

Finding Motivation When You Don't Have Inspiration

Here's where inspiration and motivation collide. You aren't always going to have inspiration to keep moving forward. The climb to your goals is sometimes unforgiving—full of bumps, weak branches and weight to hold you down. There will be moments where you feel like giving up because your inspiration has run out; this is a stage that many refer to as becoming "burnt out." It's in those moments where we need to find help from others to keep us going.

Any time I think of this scenario, I think of the show *Who Wants to Be a Millionaire?* If you've never seen the show (Where have you *been?!*), it's a gameshow that asks contestants questions that get increasingly harder as they draw closer and closer to winning—you guessed it!—a million dollars. With each question, the contestant is given four possible answers and forced to choose the correct one. If the contestant is unsure about the answer, they can use one of their "lifelines" given at the start of their journey. Back in the original version of the show, these lifelines included things like 50/50 chances (eliminating two options), phoning a friend for help or asking the audience for assistance.[3]

Isn't that the way it goes? Sometimes we find ourselves in a rut, lacking the inspiration to keep working towards our goals; our self-discipline gives way and we can't seem to find any reason to take even *one* more step forward. When that happens, you need to take a page from the contestants on *Who Wants to Be a Millionaire?* and use a lifeline. Maybe you "phone a friend" to ask for advice. Perhaps you "ask the audience" for assistance by reaching out to someone that's been actively watching you work towards your goal(s) each day; it could be a coworker, pastor, counselor, acquaintance… you name it! The point is, we all need motivation from others at some point.

Another trick for finding motivation when you lack personal drive is focusing on the *small victories*. I believe that small wins give just us as much satisfaction as accomplishing our big goals, but in a smaller time frame. For example, sales representatives have annual sales goals that they need to hit, but the brief thrill they get after they close a sale provides the same level of excitement as hitting their annual goal. Always search for the small wins, they can help you stay energized to push forward.

The Risk of "Too Much" Motivation

Motivation is an incredible tool to use when you've hit a wall while pursuing your goals; however, there's a catch to receiving too much help from other people. Despite their best intentions, others might accidentally derail you and send you down the wrong path.

In what feels like a lifetime ago, I used to be a salesman. As soon as you step into the sales industry, you hear words like "the grind," "hustle" and "outwork." There's a stereotypical expectation that all salespersons should make 80 to 100 calls a day, send over 100 emails, prospect and do drop-by appointments. Not knowing any better, when I first started out, I based my entire work day around those numbers and focused on calling and emailing as many people as possible.

There's only one problem: the client doesn't care how many calls you've made that day—the number of emails you've sent out before 9 a.m. won't convince them that they should buy from you; they only buy from those they trust.

In order to earn their trust, I needed to focus on growing the *relationship* with my clients; this meant making less calls in order to spend five to 10 minutes on the phone with interested buyers. I later found out my employer *preferred* that I made 40 calls each day instead of 80 as it meant I was too busy talking to clients to meet the call numbers.

So how does that translate to motivation? I spent many years listening to the "motivation" of a stereotypical salesman saying that I needed to call as many people as possible. What I failed to consider is that that very advice was pulling me away from achieving my sales goals.

By switching that motivation out with my own intrinsic desire to build relationships with my clients, I finally saw the sales results I'd had been chasing for many years.

III. Common Misconceptions of Self-Discipline

In order to set the vision for the goals you want to accomplish, you need to understand the definition of "self-discipline." Most people think it means that you have to have the mindset of a drill sergeant or a lion tamer; that's why so many people are turned off to the idea of it.

That's not what successful self-discipline looks like at all. Let's take some time to bust some of the most common myths (or lies) of self-discipline.

Myth #1: "Failure Won't Happen If I Have Good Self-Discipline"

I wish this was true. The fact is, even the most successful people endure failure and conflict in their lives; you will too, as will I, along with everyone else that walks this earth. We'll talk about how to battle through failure extensively in a later chapter. For now, I'm going to put on my nerd glasses and treat you to a story.

In mythology, Phoenixes are known to simultaneously go up in flames whenever they've reached the end of their lives; all that's left afterwards is a pile of ash. Sad, right? Think again! The same Phoenix that combusted is reborn again in the remains of its ashes.

The story of the Phoenix is the perfect example of how we need to approach our failures. We shouldn't expect failure to never happen; that's unrealistic. Instead—when failure *does* occur—see it as an opportunity to learn, grow and rise from the ashes of those failures as a new and improved version of yourself. Don't avoid failure; *embrace* it.

Myth #2: "Self-Discipline Provides a Completely Straight Path"

This misconception is the most toxic of all. People confuse structure with straightforwardness. Self-discipline doesn't provide you with a straight and narrow path to your goals. There will be many trials and tribulations along the way; however, self-discipline provides you with focus and training to adjust to the obstacles you come across.

Let's use our metaphorical self-discipline tree as an example. When climbing a tree, you don't just go straight up; after all, it's a tree, not a ladder. Many times you'll have to move to an adjacent branch in order to find something sturdier to help you climb to the next level. Occasionally, you might step on a branch that snaps or makes a funny sound. Do you give up? Of course not. You simply reassess your path.

That's what self-discipline can offer you as you work towards your goals; it grants you a consistent routine you can resort to when the going gets rough.

While we're talking about ladders, let me ask you this: why don't we find climbing ladders as much fun as climbing trees? Because there's no *challenge* in it. The same goes for the goals we set. If not for failure and adversity, there would be no sense of accomplishment at the end. When you set your vision for the goals you wish to achieve, don't let the potential of hardship deter you; let it *excite* you!

Myth #3: "Self-Discipline Isn't Sustainable"

This myth is the very reason I wrote this book. It pains me to know that there are people out there that don't think they have control over their own lives; they don't believe that self-discipline is renewable. They're essentially admitting defeat to the hurdles in their lives that seem too tall to jump over.

The people that believe this myth have a misconception that self-discipline is all about maximum exertion day-in and day-out. But here's the secret: self-discipline isn't about pushing out the same intensity every minute of every day, it's about finding your ideal levels of exertion for each goal you have. That way, you won't burn yourself out before you reach them. We'll talk about this more in our Well-Being Chapter.

Did you know that four out of every five Americans struggle with financial issues at some point in their lives?[4] Depending on the severity of it, overcoming their financial setbacks might seem too improbable of a task. However, Dave Ramsey—one of the most highly-regarded personal money management experts of our time—has helped millions of people climb out from *serious* amounts of debt. No matter how big or small the damage is, he always recommends that his listeners/readers/audience begin the process by taking seven baby steps.

With the first step, he recommends saving $1,000 in an emergency fund. Although the steps get progressively more intense as you go along, Dave's path to "Financial Peace" becomes increasingly easier for those who follow it for one reason: it starts small, with baby steps.[5]

If you start establishing your self-discipline with baby steps, you'll find that it becomes more natural with time. Self-discipline is meant to be scalable, not sustainable. Once you accomplish one baby step, you can move on to the next. As the great Martin Luther King Jr. once said, "You don't have to see the whole staircase, just take the first step."[6]

IV. The Power of Self-Awareness

The Sixth Sense is one of the most iconic films of all time. It follows the life of Dr. Malcolm Crowe, a Philadelphia child psychologist, whose patient, Cole Sear, has the ability to talk to the dead. We all know the famous line, "I see dead people." In one of the most dramatic plot twists in all of cinema, (spoiler alert!) it turns out that Malcolm was—to his bewilderment—dead the entire time. Talk about a shock to your system!

While you might not ever find out something *that* dramatic about yourself, you'd be surprised how little you actually know about (enter your name here) and how significant that information can be to your life. There are many traits and habits you might not even be aware of; if you had the ability to identify those, you could turn them into more positive habits. Don't worry, we'll cover that in a later chapter!

As a matter of fact, this entire book is a guide to self-assessment. All three phases: Preparation, Production and Persistence, show you how to look inward and perform a SWOT analysis of sorts to determine your **S**trengths, **W**eaknesses, **O**pportunities and **T**hreats.[7] This business tool is usually used for evaluating a company's competitive advantage. In this context, however, you can use it to evaluate yourself. Let's break it down like this:

Strengths: Your God-given gifts. Your strengths can be identified as certain qualities or talents you have that can be helpful when accomplishing your goals.

Weaknesses: The current holes in your self-discipline; things that don't come as easily to you as they might to other people. It's hard to look at our own flaws, but it's *essential* to your growth. If you pinpoint a weakness, you can pinpoint a solution. Here's an example: I'm a horrible procrastinator, but I'm able to turn that weakness into a strength by giving myself a daily outline to follow (which I'll mention in the Organization Chapter).

Opportunities: Typically factors outside of your control that grant you a potential advantage when accomplishing your goals. For example, let's say your goal is to become a manager by the end of this year. That opportunity might come through your current employer or from another organization.

Threats: Potential obstacles you'll face when you set out to accomplish your goals and dreams. Threats can be internal and external. Using the example of wanting to become a manager: externally, the company might shut down or someone else might be in the running for the management position you want. Internally, you might hit a wall at some point and lose vision of your goals; you may get discouraged and lose interest in your work. We all come across threats at some point. If you prepare yourself for them ahead of time, you can minimize the harm they cause.

V. Finding Your Definition of Success

If you're going to be successful, you first have to understand what that term means for you. What do you view as a success? Despite what today's society might tell you, success has never been a comprehensive term. If you *really* want to feel the elation of being successful, you have to know what it means.

By many people's definition, Anthony Bourdain had all the "success" that you could think of: he was a successful book author, journalist and TV personality on shows like *The Taste, A Cook's Tour* and *Anthony Bourdain: Parts Unknown.* He was beloved by fans everywhere. Tragically, he took his own life at the Le Chambard Hotel in Alsace, France, while he was on location to shoot his show.[8]

I'm not going to speculate on what led Anthony to take his own life. All I know is that you owe it to yourself and your loved ones to understand what you would define as success with each of our goals; otherwise, you'll never be satisfied.

Maybe you have a goal of losing 50 pounds by the time you and your family take a trip to the beach next summer; that's a *fantastic* goal! But what if you only lose 30 pounds by the time that trip comes around? Are you telling me you wouldn't view losing *30 pounds* as a success?

Here's my point: success shouldn't always be defined as "the point in which you accomplish your goals." That is a *dangerous* precedent, my friend. If you have a goal of graduating college with a 4.0 GPA, would you not view a 3.9 GPA (.8 higher than the average college graduate's GPA) as a huge achievement?[9]

Have you ever heard the phrase "beauty is in the eye of the beholder?" This phrase insinuates that beauty doesn't exist on its own, it's created by those that see it.

Let me tell you something, *success* is in the eye of the beholder, too. Whoever is holding the goal gets to determine whether something is successful or not. Others will certainly have their opinions about it, but what does that matter? If you determine what success is, then you can experience success. If you experience success, then you are—by the very definition of it—successful. If you're successful, then you'll find happiness with your progress, even if you haven't reached your end goal yet.

Let me end the chapter with this thought: if you don't envision moments of success with each of your goals, when will you ever find happiness? How will you ever find the strength to push through and achieve your long-term goals?

Do you want to know what the key to maintaining inspiration is? Happiness. At the end of the day, there's only one person that decides whether or not you're happy, and that's *you*. If you don't consider yourself successful or happy while you work towards your goals, you won't find happiness when you achieve them.

Make the conscious decision right now that no matter what goals you set for yourself, no matter how long they take to accomplish, you will be *happy*. You owe that to yourself!

CHAPTER 2

GOAL-SETTING

LaDainian Tomlinson (also known as 'LT') is one of my all-time favorite professional athletes. If you've never heard of him, he's a Hall of Fame running back who played the majority of his career with the San Diego Chargers. I'll never forget the day my man crush with him began.

Back in 2006, the St. Louis Rams played against the Chargers in San Diego—LT ran *all over* the Rams that day. He ended up running for 183 yards on 25 carries, two rushing touchdowns and a receiving touchdown.[1] Like I said—he ran all over the Rams that day. However, there was one play that specifically stood out from the rest.

In the first quarter, Philip Rivers (the Chargers' quarterback) handed the ball off to LT, who shot through his offensive line like a cannonball. He proceeded to stiff arm the Ram's safety so hard that the guy's helmet flew off, then ran it in for a 38-yard touchdown; he made the entire thing look effortless. I remember thinking, *"Who is this guy? I have to know more about him!"* So I jumped on the family computer and spent the rest of the game reading up on his story.

As it turns out, it's *quite* the story. Take one look at his National Football League (NFL) career highlights and you'd think he was born with the natural athletic ability that few of us are blessed with; but the truth is, LaDainian Tomlinson became a Hall of Fame running back by setting goals from the early age of six. As a matter of fact, he was so goal-oriented that, at the age of six years old, he told his mom that he would play in the NFL.[2] Talk about calling your shot!

So how does someone go about fulfilling a lofty goal they made when they were young? In his Hall of Fame speech, LaDainian attributes two major factors in achieving his goal: God and his support system—namely his mother, Loreane.

When he was 12 years old, LT spotted a flier at the Boys and Girls Club that he was a part of; it was a flier for Jay Novacek's (a tight end for the Dallas Cowboys) youth football camp. The flier mentioned that one of LT's biggest idols, legendary Cowboys running back Emmitt Smith, was scheduled to appear at the camp. Young LaDainian *begged* his mom to let him go to the camp. After raising money from her two jobs, she granted his wish. Little did she know how high of a return she would get on that investment!

At the first practice of the camp, Jay Novacek had all of the kids line up for a hand-off drill. When LT's turn came up, Emmitt Smith jumped in the line to be the one to hand the ball off to him. Later on in the camp, LaDainian had another encounter with his childhood idol when Emmitt Smith almost ran him over walking down a staircase. LT credits those two run-ins with Emmitt Smith as life-altering moments.

As a child, Tomlinson struggled severely with his self-confidence. After what could only have been a few cumulative minutes with his boyhood role model, he left the camp believing that he really *could* achieve his dream of playing in the NFL one day. However, that wasn't the only goal/dream that he ended up having. In fact, he added more goals to the pile on his road to the NFL.

While he played football at Texas Christian University (TCU), he made a goal to turn around a Horned Frogs football program from a one-win team his freshmen year to a 10-2 record his senior season.[3] After he was drafted by the Chargers (and completed his lifelong dream), he set his eyes on winning a Super Bowl and making it into the NFL's Hall of Fame. These days, his goal is to make a difference in both football and society.

In the closing moments of his Hall of Fame induction speech in 2017, LaDainian pointed out the beauty of the potential we all have in front of us by saying, "Football is a microcosm of America. All races, religions, and creeds living, playing and competing side by side."

He also went on to say that, "America is the land of opportunity. Let's not slam the doors on those who may look or sound different from us; Rather, let's open it wide for those who believe in themselves that anything is possible and are willing to compete and take whatever risk necessary to work hard and succeed."

As LT points out here, everyone's story is different; I won't pretend to know the circumstances that you battle through every day. But I know this—LaDainian had some *very* big hurdles to jump over on his way to fulfilling a goal he made when he was no older than a first grader. *If he can do it, so can you.*

In order to accomplish your goals, you first need to *set* them. I know you've set millions of goals in your life, but I'm here to challenge you on that!

In this chapter, we're going to uncover what proper goal-setting looks like when paired with successful self-discipline. We'll cover how to structure your short-and-long-term goals, how to make your goals achievable and the best way to see where your priorities lie.

It's my firm belief that no worthwhile goal occurs without a defining moment. Let's start by identifying what defining moments look like, how you can recognize them and why you should *lean* into them whenever they occur.

I. Discovering Your Defining Moment

Many times in life, there comes a point where you realize that you've strayed away from your path. This can occur in any facet of your life: your faith, your family, your finances, your career, your personal life, you name it! In those moments, you can choose to do one of two things: 1) Continue with your current patterns and behaviors or 2) Force yourself to make a change.

These are what are referred to as *defining moments*. These moments will urge you to ask yourself "why," they will challenge your current thought process and push you to make a change in your life.[4] That change often comes in the form of setting new goals for yourself. When these defining moments happen, they can *rock* your world. It wasn't too long ago that I had one of my own!

In October of 2020, life hit me *hard*, but in a good way. My wife Bre and I had just had our first child—our son, Asher—and our worlds were completely flipped upside-down. The regular and successful routines we'd set for ourselves were thrown out the window. Nothing else was more of a priority than being there for that little boy.

I love what I do for work, but it isn't ideal for raising a child. I'm currently a Freelance Writer, which means I get paid for the articles I produce—I don't get compensated for the work until the article is finalized and approved.

Before Asher, I was writing seven articles a day. Each article took around 45 minutes to an hour to finish, meaning I was working at least six cumulative hours a day. Compare that to the average salaried worker who, research shows, is only productive for two hours and 53 minutes in an eight-hour work day.[5] Based off those statistics, I'm over twice as productive as the average worker. I take great pride in that!

After Ash was born, I took a week off. When I got back to work, however, I found that my worst nightmare had come to pass—I was *exhausted*. The first week back was the most difficult work week of my life. That Friday afternoon, I had just finished a frustrating day at work, so I planned to reward myself by going to the bookstore to get the next book in a fictional series I was enjoying at the time. Once I logged off from work, I kissed my wife and my son before heading out the door.

To be completely transparent, I started crying as soon as I got in my car. I remember driving to the bookstore and asking myself, "What are you *doing* with your career?" At that moment, I realized how unsustainable my job was. Was I going to write seven articles every day for the rest of my life? As much as I enjoyed writing articles, I needed to do something I could get more *fulfillment* out of; also, something that could help me provide for my wife, son and any other children we might have. Was I going to write *eight* or *nine* articles a day? Not a chance!

At that moment, I opted to make a change, but I wasn't sure where to start— so I began to pray to God for guidance. After I finished praying, I scolded myself some more for *other* areas of my life in which I was frustrated with for my lack of progress. Once that was done, I prayed again and asked God to give me direction through my action. I asked myself, *"What do you want to achieve? What skills do you have to help people?"* I didn't have an answer. That's when I decided to grab a self-help book while at the bookstore, the first step I made towards change.

There's one thing I want to clarify—we're talking about *defining* moments, not "Aha!" moments. Sometimes, you can go through a defining moment without having a firm idea of your next steps. During *my* defining moment, I didn't have a clue of what to do next; all I needed was to accept that drastic changes needed to be made. A few weeks later, my "Aha!" moment came while I was listening to a marketing podcast in which the host encouraged listeners to write a book—the rest is history!

Here's my point: the defining moments lead to "Aha!" moments. Without a defining moment, your mind won't be receptive to the opportunities and ideas around you. Whenever those defining moments happen, there's a self-audit process that needs to take place; that way, you can assess your current situation and the potential opportunities that can help you right the ship.

Here are a few questions you can ask yourself whenever you feel a need to make a change:

a. Why are you upset or frustrated with your current predicament?

b. How did you get here?

c. Who is to blame? (Hint: *you* are. It's important to acknowledge that.)

d. What can you do to correct it?

e. Where do you go from here?

I'll give you an example of how this works. Let's say that John Doe's defining moment comes one day when he takes a look in the mirror with his shirt off. He steps on the scale and realizes he's gained 50 pounds. He could choose to do one of two things: 1) Keep up his current workout and eating habits or 2) Opt to start losing the weight. In that moment, he can ask himself these questions to search for answers:

a. Why are you frustrated, John?
Because I let myself get to this point. I let other aspects of my life affect my health. I'm not satisfied with the way I look. I'm losing self-confidence.

b. How did you get here, John?

I started ignoring my health. I let the stress of my life affect my diet. I started making excuses for why I couldn't go to the gym. I stopped prioritizing my physical well-being.

c. Who is to blame, John?
I am.

d. What can you do to correct it, John?
I'm going to start focusing more on my exercise and nutrition. I'm going to begin to prioritize my health over other areas of my life that I deem less important.

e. Where do you go from here, John?
I'm going to commit to working out three times a week, to start. I'm going to download an app to help me track my calories each day. I'm going to cut down on snack times. I'm going to eat more vegetables.

Notice the intent behind our hypothetical friend's last two answers. He didn't say "I could" or "I might." He said "I'm going to," as if it's a pre-conceived action: it's going to happen—John Doe *will* take back control of his life.

Whatever your defining moment looks like, it's best to be honest with yourself, especially if you won't like the answers you hear. Trust me, you *need* to hear them.

Perhaps you've already had your defining moment and are now looking for answers. If so, start with these questions. If you answer them honestly, I *promise* that you'll find directions on where to start.

If you haven't had your defining moment yet, it will come! You never know when one could appear. My defining moment came at a moment of frustration with my career. LaDainian Tomlinson's came at a moment of elation after meeting his childhood idol.

Defining moments come in many different shapes and sizes. Be receptive to them, keep an open mind and *lean* into them when they occur.

II. Short-Term and Long-Term Goals

When I sent out my self-discipline questionnaire to my list of well-established professionals, about one-third of my questions were focused on the topic of goal-setting: I wanted to see how they created their goals and what ways they set themselves up for success. All but one—count it, *one*—of the responses I received had the same answer: they set their long-term goals first, then established short-term goals that could help them achieve the long-term goals they set.

In other words, they viewed their long-term goals as the "big project" in their lives. They subconsciously deemed these goals as achievable, yet lofty. In order to make their long-term goals obtainable, they built short-term goals that rally around the effort of executing their biggest dreams in life. I find that *fascinating!*

Those that answered my questionnaire were in a variety of fields such as finance, professional sports, therapy, science, sales, merchandising, engineering, human resources, education, customer service, copywriting, construction, marketing, product development, real estate, land acquisition, logistics, nursing, pastoring, insurance and coaching. All of them are successful, and all but one of them constructed their habits the same way.

They compartmentalize their long-term goals; they break their dreams into bite-sized portions. If one of their dreams is represented in the form of our self-discipline tree, they break that big-time goal up branch by branch. Let's take a deeper dive at this successful form of goal-setting.

Intertwining Your Long-Term and Short Term Goals

Based on the statistics I gathered from the answers to my questionnaires, I found that 98-percent of successful people established their long-term goals first; they envisioned the tree they wanted to climb, and set their eyes on the very top. That fact cannot be overstated.

Why do the most successful people set their long-term goals first? Because long-term goals are life-altering; they're the measure of how intrinsically-motivated people gauge their life output. Just to be clear, not all of the long-term goals my survey-takers set were tied into their careers; in fact, *very* few of them were. How refreshing is that?

I came across goals such as getting married to their girlfriend, losing 75 pounds, becoming entirely debt-free, traveling to 10 different places within three years and everything in between. What does this tell us? That successful people don't stop at goal-setting for their professional life; they use it in every aspect of their lives—if not, more so!

So what is the ideal timeline for these goals? To put it another way: how far out should you set your long-term goals and short-term goals for? To be honest, the answer depends on the goal.

If you have a goal of becoming the CEO of your company, then, by all means, you should pursue it! However, if you're currently in an entry-level position, you should plan a timeline that's significantly longer than the typical goal-accomplishing timeline.

Nothing's impossible, but rewards tend to favor the realistic. With that said, modern research has shown that goals are more likely to be reached when you set long-term goals with a three to five-year timeline, and short-term goals with a six-month to three-year timeline.[6]

So how realistic or lofty should your goals be? As it turns out, the loftiness of your goals hardly—remember that I said *hardly*— affects whether you have a chance of achieving them; the fact that you've set your goals already gives you an advantage.

Back in 1979, Harvard University performed a study on their graduating class. They asked each graduate this question:

"Have you set written goals and created a plan for their attainment?"

It was determined that *84-percent* of the graduating class had not set any goals at all; 13-percent of them had set some goals, but didn't have any plans to achieve them and only three percent of the graduating class had written down their goals *and* established a plan to obtain them. So, if you take the time to write down your goals and devise a way to achieve them, you're already ahead of 84-percent of Harvard graduates back in 1979. *Congratulations!*

While those statistics are pretty eye-opening, here's another one for you: the 13-percent who had written their goals down without a plan of action were making *twice* as much as the 84-percent that didn't.

Here's the *real* shocker, the three percent who had written down their goals *and* made a plan brought in over *ten times* as much as the 84-percent that hadn't taken the time to write down their goals.[7] I imagine you're reaching for a piece of paper and a pencil right now! The point here is to simply take the time to *set* your goals and write them down.

When you take the time to write out your long-term and short-term goals, you're doing *exactly* what the three percent of that Harvard graduating class did: you're establishing goals (long-term goals) and writing down plans to achieve them (short-term goals). Make sense?

Learning to Ride It Out

Now that we've talked about the importance of *writing* your goals out, let's talk about the importance of *riding* your goals out. Yes, the similar sound of those two phrases *was* intentional!

While you write out your goals, it's important to understand the path that lies ahead of you; there will be obstacles, there will be bumps and more than likely, there will be failures as well. So are you just going to pack up when those occur? Of course, not! Your ability to battle through the adversity of your goals is won or lost in the *Preparation Phase*.

Yes, envision yourself crossing the finish line. But also envision yourself pushing through the fatigue halfway through that marathon.

Yes, imagine yourself becoming an All-American in your sport. But also imagine the workouts and sacrifices it will take to give yourself a leg up on the competition.

Yes, visualize yourself becoming entirely debt-free. But also visualize the financial sacrifices you have to make— such as not going out with friends or not spending money on clothes— to pay off those loans. This isn't considered negative thinking; it's called *setting the expectation*, and it's an important piece to the puzzle.

Once you set the expectation, you'll be able to ride out the setbacks. There will be things you didn't plan for. There will be moments you'll want to quit. There will even be different opportunities you'll be tempted to jump on that could derail you from your goal; don't let them. Like the REO Speedwagon song, you need to "ride the storm out."

To paint a better picture of why riding it out is so crucial, allow me to use a baseball analogy. Let's imagine that a batter on your favorite Major League Baseball team (go Cardinals!) is stepping up to the plate. These days, it isn't often that the batter will see too many fastballs thrown right down the middle of the strike zone. The pitcher he's facing is likely to throw him other pitches with movement, such as a curveball, slider, sinker or some other pitch that's harder to get a hit off of.

If the batter goes up there and swings at every curveball the pitcher throws, he'll strike out the majority of the time. The key to batting isn't swinging at the first three pitches thrown at you; it's all about taking a few curveballs to wait for the fastball which—in this context—refers to the opportunity that you've planned for.

Life isn't just going to throw you fastballs down the middle of the plate; it's actually more likely to throw you curveballs. What are you prepared to do about that? Are you going to swing at those off-speed pitches and risk striking out on your goals? Or are you going to sit (not swing) on those curveballs in order to wait for the fastball that you can knock out of the park? If I had to guess, I'd say you're more interested in doing the latter!

III. The Art of SMART

Now that we've uncovered the importance of using your short-term goals to chip away at your long-term goals, writing and the riding them out, let's switch our focus here. How can we put all of that within reach? How can we set our goals in a way that they become more visible and within our grasp? One of the most helpful ways I've found is by using the SMART goal method.

Originally created by George T. Doran in 1981 and readopted by many well-respected professionals in the psychology field, the SMART goal method is an outline to ensure your goals—whether long-term or short-term—are credible.

SMART is an acronym that stands for **S**pecific, **M**easurable, **A**chievable, **R**elevant and **T**ime-Based.[8] Each of these are to be seen as prerequisites for your goals. Let's take a closer look at each of them:

SPECIFIC - Think in terms of *detail*. Avoid having general goals. What are you hoping to achieve? Why does this goal mean so much to you? Where will this goal be accomplished? What do you need to emerge victorious with this goal?

MEASURABLE - Think in *increments*. How can you quantify the goal you want to achieve? How many steps are involved in it? What do those steps look like? Measuring your goals allows you to track your progress as you work towards achieving them.

ACHIEVABLE - Think about goals that are *realistic*. When you list out a goal, ask yourself how you will be able to accomplish it. What events or activities can bring you closer to achieving this goal? Don't confuse achievable for "easy." That is *not* the idea, here; it's about setting goals that are within your grasp or that *could* be within your grasp if you take a certain path, such as getting your realtor's license to become a real estate agent.

RELEVANT - Think in terms of *growth*. Every goal you set should be aimed towards self-improvement. Your goals should be worth the sacrifice and commitment you're going to make to achieve them. You don't want to have reached the top of your tree, look down and say to yourself *"This wasn't worth the effort."* Is this the right time for you to act on this goal? How does it fit in with the other goals you have?

TIME-BASED - Think in terms of *deadlines*. Separate your long-term and short-term goals into time increments. How can you make progress towards these goals every year? Every month? Every week? Every day? It might seem tedious, but I guarantee you, if you take the time to map out a way to work towards your goals each day, you'll start to gain real momentum towards achieving them in no time!

I hope that each of these steps are useful to you. I often find—and my survey answers confirmed this—that people use two or three of these when setting their goals, but rarely do they use all five. Let me tell you this: it takes all five to create an actionable plan.

I'll give you an example. Let's use six-year-old LT's goal to assess how *"smart"* of a goal it was (sorry, couldn't help myself!). You remember the one— "When I grow up, I'm going to play in the NFL." How does the SMART goal-setting apply to his statement? Let's see for ourselves:

SPECIFIC - There are two specificities to young LaDainian's goal: First, that he'd play in the NFL—not the MLB, not the National Basketball Association. More importantly, his goal didn't stop at the National Collegiate Athletic Association. Secondly, he wanted to get drafted and play in the pros. I don't have proof of this, but if he mentioned he was going to be a running back, that would be considered another "specific" aspect of his goal.

MEASURABLE - How would little LT know when he accomplished his goal? The first time an NFL quarterback handed the ball off to him in a regular season game.

ACHIEVABLE - This is the perfect example of making an achievable goal. Studies have shown that a high-schooler's chances of making it to the NFL is only .08 percent.[9] *Less than one percent*; certainly not an easy goal. How did LT make it achievable? By playing high school ball and getting recruited. Then he blew NFL scouts away at TCU and got drafted, making his NFL dream all the more achievable along the way.

RELEVANT - This might be the easiest one to answer. LT's goal was relevant because football was his whole world. All of his other goals—go to college, get bigger and stronger, go to Jay Novacek's youth football camp—were all a byproduct of achieving this dream.

TIME-BASED - He would (and did) achieve this goal when he grew up, when he graduated from college and was old enough to be drafted in the NFL draft (around the age of 21 to 22, if young LT was getting age-specific with his goals).

Now, was young LT intentionally using the SMART goal-setting method when he made that declaration to his mom? Probably not; but that's not the point. The point is that when you set goals that appease all five of these factors, whether you do so intentionally or not, you give yourself a legitimate shot to fulfill those dreams.

Think back to any of the monumental goals you've achieved in your life and I'll bet you can find ways in which these five factors contributed to the success you had.

IV. Finding Your Priorities

I know what you're thinking, *"What if my tree takes longer to climb than I had expected?"* Many people hesitate to give themselves time-based goals because of how quickly life can change. For example, if you had a goal of starting a business by the summer of 2020, that plan was likely faltered by the worldwide COVID-19 pandemic. But let me ask you this: does that line of thinking help you in any way? Does your fear of the unknown have any effect on whether or not something unforeseen occurs? Not at all. Here's another question for you: so what?

Maybe your goal of becoming a manager gets pushed back when someone else gets the open management position instead of you. So what?

Perhaps your goal of becoming debt-free gets thwarted when your spouse's car breaks down and you're forced to take out an auto loan. So what?

Do those dreams become any less realistic because they didn't happen at the *exact* time you'd planned? Nope. I promise you that it will feel just as sweet—if not more so—when you finally accomplish them. I'm a huge fan of time-based goals, which is the main reason I'm focusing on short-term and long-term goals so heavily.

Set a firm date for when your goals will be accomplished and they'll become that much more likely to be achieved; I truly believe that. The time-based aspect acts more as a measure of accountability than it does a make-or-break deadline. There are obviously a few exceptions to that, but the goal doesn't often vanish from thin air if you aren't able to meet the time-based aspect of it. I encourage you to keep that in mind!

However, let's take the time component out of it for a second. What do we have left when we do that? We have goals that could be defined as either small goals or big goals. How is that helpful? It removes the pressure of the time-projected element to your goals while you prioritize them.

By establishing small goals and big goals, you can focus more on the *subject* of the goals, rather than how it fits in your calendar. It can also help you uncover the subliminal priority of those goals. The main objective, right now, is to get all those goals you've thought of out of your head and onto a piece of paper. I have a great exercise to help you do that—I call it the Personal Priority List!

The Personal Priority List

All my Type-A people that are reading this, I urge you to bear with me; this exercise is meant to help you in three ways.

First, it will help you write down the goals you want to achieve, possibly for the first time ever. Second, it will help you understand where your priorities lie in life, and whether you need to change them. Third, it will help you accomplish your goals through the uncertainty of life.

I promise this will be worth it. This is the exact method I used to write down my goals—one of which was writing this book! You're literally reading proof that this exercise works wonders.

Start by grabbing a piece of paper and a pen at the very beginning of your day. It's very important that you grab a *pen,* not a *pencil* (think permanence!). Once you have those two things, start writing down every goal that comes to your mind. If you're anything like me, you'll draw a blank the first time you go to write down your goals—and that's okay! Take that pen and paper with you everywhere you go. When a goal comes to your mind, write it down. Try to leave at least half an inch between each goal (so they're easier to interpret for the next step).

Once you feel like all of your goals are listed on the paper, open up Microsoft Word or the Notes app on your phone and list them in terms of priority, *not* time. Which one do you want to accomplish the most? Place those at the top and work your way down until each goal on your paper is accounted for.

Now that you have your list, let's place each of them into one of three categories: Personal, Professional and Family. Enter in a dash at the end of each goal, then enter in the category in which they fall under. Here's an example:

1. Bench Press 225 lbs Ten Times — Personal
2. Finish Writing My Book— Professional
3. Take Two Family Vacations This Year— Family

You can also use the table on the next page to list each goal under the category it falls into. Once each of your goals has been put into one of the three categories, count up the amount of goals you have for each one. When I did my Personal Priority List, I had a total of 24 goals: nine personal goals, six professional goals and nine family goals. This is where you might have a reckoning of where your priorities lie.

Just to clarify, there isn't a right or wrong combination here. If you currently have many more professional goals than family goals, you shouldn't feel guilty about that; that might not always be the case. People's priorities change all the time. With that said, if you don't like the way your priorities fall, try adding more goals that are relevant to the category of your life in which you *want* to prioritize.

Remember the surveys I did? There was another common theme among most of the answers: a majority of the respondents admitted that they wished they'd prioritize their personal and family goals as much as they did their professional goals.

Once you know how your priorities are listed, you can structure your day around them, which we'll cover in the next chapter. Speaking of, hold on to that Personal Priority List you just made; we'll be using it again for a fun tool that I've created at the end of the next chapter on Organization.

Now let's go get organized!

Personal Priority List

Personal	Professional	Family

Chapter 3

ORGANIZATION

Organization is relative to the person arranging it. I've met people at the top of their field who have pigsties for desks, but do their job flawlessly. Even Albert Einstein, one of the most influential physicists in our history, was apparently a *massive* slob.

One of my biggest professional mentors practically lives out of his office; he has snacks in his drawers, multiple pairs of shoes under his desk and a pile of promotional items so tall, you'd think he was attempting to build a totem pole. But it works for him! He knows exactly where anything is at any given time.

I'll never forget the day I asked him if he had any Wite-Out. He stood up from his desk, walked to the other corner of his office, moved a pile of items, opened a drawer, grabbed two items and asked me, "BIC or Paper Mate?"

To anyone else that saw his office, things probably looked out of sorts; but in his eyes, everything was right where it was supposed to be. This is how we should organize our goals. Everything doesn't have to be perfect. The timelines don't have to fit perfectly for you to achieve more than one objective simultaneously. If you wait for the stars to align, I'll bet that you can only achieve one or two goals in your lifetime. We need to learn how to organize the goals we've set so that we can take actionable steps to accomplish them.

In many ways, organizing your goals makes them more attainable; it helps you to get inside the goal and figure out what needs to happen, and when. In this chapter, we are going to take a deeper dive into how organizing your goals can give you the momentum to take that first step. Then the second one. Then the third one.

We'll talk through how to effectively manage your time, handle multiple goals at once, and—my personal favorite—how to achieve work-life balance.

Organization is *key* to your success. The uniformity of your goals is entirely up to you. If you're a perfectionist that craves order and diligence, then by all means organize your goals as such. But let me warn you: your opportunities don't often happen in the order you want them to; sometimes you just have to go with the flow.

Accomplishing a goal always begins the same way: with Day One. Let's jump into time management techniques so that you can learn how to organize Day One and maximize it right away!

I. Time Management

Have you heard of chronotypes before? They refer to the internal clocks that all humans have. These clocks have a direct effect on the way your body is naturally productive; the timing of it is everything.

According to Dr. Michael Breus—a sleep specialist—every person's internal clock can be categorized into one of four chronotypes: Wolves, Bears, Lions and Dolphins.[1] Each of them have different characteristics and sleep patterns. The main benefit of knowing your chronotype is identifying when you should go to sleep and *how long* you need to sleep to maximize your productivity the following day. However, there are many other perks to knowing your chronotype; it can help you identify when you should eat, work out, be productive and organize your day. For those of you that are interested, his book, *The Power of When*, can help you further understand your internal clock.

I, for example, fall under the Bear chronotype; this means that my productivity and sleep schedule is *heavily* tied to the hours the sun is up/down, and further, I need eight hours of sleep each night. But here's the crazy part I discovered: a Bear chronotype's least productive point in the day is between the 2 p.m. to 3 p.m. window. I realized—in the following days after reading that for the first time—how true that actually is for me. Now I make sure that I have a full cup of black coffee on my desk for my afternoon shift of writing.

Listen, I'm not telling you that you *have* to go find out what your chronotype is; that's not the point I'm trying to make. Here's my point: in order to achieve successful self-discipline, you *have* to master the art of daily time management. Your day should be scheduled down to each and every hour. Why? Because this provides you with accountability. It also ensures that you have enough time to work towards your professional, personal and family goals each day.

Remember that Personal Priority List you made at the end of Chapter 2? It's time to pull that out again! Use it as a guide to schedule your day. While you plan each hour out, I want you to also focus on giving yourself time for two things: time for deep concentration and time for short breaks—as well as a lunch break, of course. Make sure you have at least 30 minutes for deep concentration on your personal goals, family goals, and professional goals.

I wouldn't be much of a leader if I didn't practice what I preach in my own life. As I previously mentioned, my job requires me to write seven articles a day. Needless to say, I have to break down my day into *very* tight compartments to achieve that goal at the end of each work day. I find that breaking down my day by the hour has helped me to accomplish daily tasks and work towards accomplishing future ones as well. Allow me to show you what my current schedule looks like at the time of writing this book. I hope that this helps inspire you to create a similar daily time management schedule to achieve your goals in life.

7 a.m.: Wake up, pray, make coffee, set up my first article of the day

8 a.m.: Finish first article, finish a chore around the house

9 a.m.: Finish second article, work on family-related task (budget, pay bills, etc.)

10 a.m.: Finish third article, prepare workout routine for the day, make pre-workout drink

11 a.m.: Finish fourth article, be in the gym by noon

Noon: Work out, be home by 1 pm

1 p.m.: Shower, have lunch, listen to a podcast, play with my son

2 p.m.: Finish fifth article, perform a family-related task

3 p.m.: Finish sixth article, make edits my clients have requested

4 p.m.: Finish seventh article, work on my book

5 p.m.: Write two pages for my book, play fetch outside with my dog

6 p.m.: Done with work for the day. Anything other than work can wait until tomorrow

7 p.m. to 9 p.m.: Eat dinner with my family, hang out with my wife and son

10 p.m.: Be in bed by this time, read 10 pages of a self-help book, gradually fall asleep

As you can see, I've locked down my work days into air-tight compartments. Doing so helps ensure that I'm getting the most out of every single day. By the time I lay my head on the pillow at night, I *know* I've worked efficiently towards my professional, personal and family goals.

Is this how I'm going to structure my work days for the rest of my life? Probably not. As my life changes, so can my schedule. I know some of you are thinking, "*Well I don't have a freelance career like you do!*" I promise you, this can still be done no matter what occupation you have. As long as you prioritize moments of deep concentration for each three goal categories, you'll find yourself enjoying the daily process *a lot* more. That, I can guarantee you!

The last thing I want to stress with your daily schedule is that you need to allow for some *flexibility*. You need to create realistic expectations for yourself, while also being able to go with the flow. Your entire day shouldn't feel destroyed if a meeting pops up that you weren't expecting; just subconsciously adjust your routine for that day and carry on! And just because one thing complicates your professional schedule doesn't mean it has to complicate your personal and family schedules too.

Whatever schedule you concoct, make sure to write it down. You won't get this on the first try; it will take several revisions for that to happen. I must've gone through 20 different iterations before coming up with my current schedule. Don't get discouraged, reader! Keep implementing new things. Focus on your goals as you make your schedule and everything else will fall into place!

II. Handling Multiple Responsibilities

The Chief Operating Officer from a previous employer of mine, we'll call him "Chad," has the most legendary rags to riches story of all time. While attending college, he made ends meet by working part-time; however, the only part-time work in his preferred field—the hotel industry—was located in a city several hours away from campus. As soon as his Friday classes were over, he'd jump into his car and drive all the way to his job, working the entire weekend to cumulate 30+ hours of work, if not more.

One weekend, a few big wigs from a well-known sports concessions company were in town for a convention. They were greeted by Chad who was working the front desk. After getting them set up with their room keys, he decided to go the extra mile by helping them carry their luggage to their respective rooms. The VIPs politely thanked him and wished him well.

Later that night, those same VIPs decided to unwind from a long day and eat at the hotel restaurant. After ordering dinner, they were surprised to see that Chad was the one serving them their food. "Aren't you the guy that checked us in?" One of the VIPs asked. "Yes sir," Chad replied, "but I overheard some of my buddies in the kitchen saying they could use an extra set of hands, so I thought I'd help out!" The big wigs complimented his tenacity, then sent him off so they could enjoy their dinner.

That same night, one of the VIPs called down to the front desk to request a few extra towels. Can you guess who wound up delivering those towels to him? That's right! Our boy, Chad. Legend has it that the big wigs were so impressed with this college kid's work ethic and flexibility that they offered him his first full-time position before he even walked the stage at graduation. He ended up climbing the ladder at that company, which is a huge reason he has the position he does today!

Handling multiple responsibilities is one of the hardest things to do in life. Whether it requires you to wear several different hats at work like Chad did, or balance your attention between your work life and personal life simultaneously, the stress of it all can pull you apart—if you let it.

But let's not look at it that way. Instead, let's look at it from a positive perspective. Let's look at it for what it really is—an opportunity to improve! There are greater rewards waiting for those that learn to juggle multiple tasks at once and produce positive results for each task. To put it another way, handling several tasks at once helps you to gain a new skillset in multiple categories.

My college lacrosse head coach had an analogy for this that I'll never forget: An employer is handed the resumes of two different college graduates. One of the graduates had a 4.0 GPA and poured his heart and soul into studying in the hopes of graduating at the top of his class. The other graduate had a 3.0 cumulative GPA, but was also a four-year student-athlete who knew how to play the piano AND was a Resident Assistant in his dorm for three years. You can probably guess where I'm going with this, right? I'd dare to say that nine times out of 10, the employer is going with the student-athlete who learned to balance his time and effort in several different responsibilities at once.

Back when I worked for the Tampa Bay Buccaneers, I was hired to work as an Account Executive in their satellite office in Sarasota. While it was a challenge at times and I didn't have the luxury of rolling up to work every day at the Bucs' headquarters—the AdventHealth Training Center—I wouldn't trade it for the world.

For many people in the Sarasota area, I was the face of the franchise. For all intents and purposes, my manager, my coworkers,and I were collectively the sales team, the marketing team, the public relations team, the events team, the networking team, the customer support team and the merchandising team. While my title said I only worked in Sales, I actually wore *each* of those previously mentioned hats every day for years.

That position taught me something I'll carry with me everywhere I go: you can't handle multiple responsibilities successfully without effective time management. You have to commit *meaningful* time to each goal/task. After you've dedicated certain time slots to your tasks, all that's left to do is put in the work! You know how to do *that* part.

I'll share one last secret I found to handle multiple responsibilities successfully: once you're done with one task, clear it from your mind and move on to the next one. Climb your self-discipline tree one branch at a time, ladies and gentlemen. Whatever goal you're working towards in that time slot, give it all you've got!

III. Debunking Work-Life Balance

If I'm being completely transparent with you, this might be the topic that I'm most passionate about. In my mind, not enough people have their priorities straight; their love lives falter because they're too obsessed with their jobs; they wind up scaring their loved ones away while trying to pursue a goal that isn't worth achieving without someone—loved ones—to celebrate it with.

In her book *The Top Five Regrets of Dying*, Bronnie Ware—a former nurse who used to tend to patients that were in the last 12 weeks of their lives—listed the five most common regrets that her patients had confessed to:

1. I wish I'd lived the life I wanted to, not the one that was expected of me.

2. I wish I hadn't worked so much.

3. I wish I'd expressed my feelings more.

4. I wish I'd stayed in touch with my friends more often.

5. I wish I'd been happier.[2]

To me, all five of those "I wishes" are essentially saying, "I wish I had prioritized work-life balance!" It's tough, isn't it? Our priorities change with each different phase of our life. The Personal Priorities List you created in the last chapter isn't the same as the one you'll create even one to two years down the road.

Here's one thing I beg you to do: stop calling it "work-life balance." For one, your "life" should always be put ahead of "work," even in a silly little phrase. Secondly, to say the world "balance" makes you think that there is an equal level you can achieve to your personal, professional and family goals—there isn't. That will never happen. It's up to you to decide which one is the most important, then prioritize it ahead of the others.

I'll give you an example. I'd say I currently have five priorities in my life:

1) Grow my relationship with God
2) Grow my relationship with my wife
3) Grow my relationship with my son
4.) Finish writing—and publishing—this book
5.) Provide for my family (through my writing)

If I *actually* managed to achieve "work-life balance" with all five of those goals, I'd only be giving each of them 20-percent of my effort. God doesn't deserve only 20-percent. My wife and son certainly don't deserve only 20-percent. Heck, my readers of this book—thank you, by the way!—deserve way more than 20-percent. On the contrary, I feel strongly that 20-percent is *way* too much effort to put on my career.

Have I found the perfect blend for managing these five priorities? Not in the slightest. *But*, I do know this: I'll never evenly disperse my efforts among them; they change with time.

Instead, let's call this what it is: life-work variation. I *love* the way one of my survey-takers—and one of my dearest friends—phrased it:

> **"I don't have any grand goals of power, or respect, or gaining a certain title within my career. Yes, I want to continue to progress in my career—and will bust my butt in order to do so—but to me, there always comes an end to the work day. Family and friends are forever."**

He makes such a great point, doesn't he? There will always be a fire inside us to find purpose in our careers; it's part of how we find our self-worth. That level of desire fluctuates from person to person. However, there is a time and place for it. Are you willing to sacrifice moments with your family and friends that you'll never get back in order to advance in your career faster? I know *I'm* not! I promise you, putting your life ahead of your work won't put a halt to your career. If it does, then you're working for the wrong company!

The guy that I just quoted? He does *very* well for himself. He's currently climbing the ranks in his company, so I'd say this method of thinking is working out well for him!

Putting your life goals ahead of your work goals will actually help you accomplish both faster. Exercising is a prime example of this! A study performed by Leeds Metropolitan University found that employees who visited the gym that day found it easier to manage their time, were far more productive *and* had more positive conversations with their coworkers/managers.[3] We'll talk more about exercise in the next phase of the book, but that study proves my point. Putting your life goals (aka your family goals and personal goals) ahead of your work goals (professional goals) will help breed better results. Am I advocating that you become selfish? Not at all. I'm encouraging you to get control of your life before life takes control of *you*.

So how do we begin to achieve this mindset? It starts with identifying the aspects of life that are most important to you.

I always have four aspects of life that are most important to me: my faith, my family, my fitness and my work; that order *never* changes for me, nor should it.

What are the top aspects of *your* life? It's up to you to consciously identify them so that you can nurture them. No matter where life takes you, you can *protect* those aspects to stay happy—you owe that to yourself!

Now, how can we make sure we're keeping that mindset while accomplishing the goals we've set for ourselves? You have to make a habit loop for it! Let me explain that a bit.

I'm a *huge* advocate for the book *The Power of Habit* by Charles Duhigg. In the book, Charles explains that every habit we develop in our lives—from brushing our teeth to the way we diet and everything in between—is developed from what he calls a "habit loop." A habit loop is a neurological loop in your brain that sits at the center of every habit in your life, whether positive or negative. The habit loop always consists of three key parts: a cue, a routine and a reward, specifically in that order. The more times you perform that habit loop, the more that habit is driven into your brain.[4]

I'll give you an example: I wake up the same way every work day. I wake up, I do an hour of work and then I have a cup of coffee. Why? I don't know. But it produces amazing results for me! In that scenario, here is my habit loop:

The Cue — My alarm clock going off
The Routine — Diving into an hour of work
The Reward — The cup of coffee I get after the first hour has passed

I've been performing this habit for so long that I don't even think about it anymore. That's not to say I don't think about the work I'm doing, but the cadence of that habit comes so naturally to me these days.

Now that we know what a habit loop is, let's create a habit loop for accomplishing the goals you've placed on your Personal Priority List!

First, identify a cue that you can use for accomplishing these goals—something that kick-starts you into focus and helps you work towards the goals you've created.

Second, identify the routine for accomplishing those goals. How can you start production towards your goals? What tasks can you perform to help you work your way towards the finish line? In my example above, my routine includes things such as performing research for my writing, making edits, creating content and so on.

Third, establish a reward program for the goals that you achieve. I have the perfect tool for this! I call it a "Bing-Goal Board," and you're going to think that it's awesome. Let's dive into that now!

IV. Bing-Goal Board

"So what is the deal with this Bing-Goal Board thing?" you might ask. To put it simply, it's a way to reward yourself for achieving your goals. I like to call it *reward*

accountability—holding yourself accountable to celebrate all of your hard work. As the name would imply, this board is a variation of a Bingo board—free space and all. It has five rows and five columns, giving you 24 spaces to fill—since the *free space* takes up one spot.

Remember that Personal Priority List you made in the last chapter? We're going to use that handy list of 24 goals that you listed on the Bing-Goal Board! Place each of those goals in the 24 spots on your board; try to do these at random, or at least separate the different categories—personal, professional and family— as much as possible.

After you achieve one of your goals, you get to cross it off your board—just as you would in Bingo. You get the idea! Whenever you cross off five goals in a row, you get to reward yourself. I find it helpful to list a few rewards right away. For example, rewarding yourself with a nice dinner at a fancy restaurant, getting tickets to the local sports team's next home game (in nicer seats than you'd usually purchase), attending a play at the local theater and so on. Whatever you view as a legitimate reward, go and do it!

See the figure on the following page for an example of our Bing-Goal Board.

CLIMBING YOUR SELF-DISCIPLINE TREE

Bing-Goal Board

		FREE SPACE		

Rewards are a *vital* piece to the puzzle. Is achieving the goal itself a reward? Sure, but the incremental accomplishments need to be honored. As I mentioned earlier, rewards complete the habit loop; without them, you can't form healthy habits. Rewards and prizes are especially helpful in completing the smaller goals that you've set—they can help you develop positive work habits that you start to do without thought.

You might be wondering, "*Is there such thing as TOO BIG of a reward?*" That's up to you to decide! I'd argue that you shouldn't overextend yourself financially to do it. My wife and I set money aside specifically to be used for our Bing-Goal Board rewards. That way, whenever we get five goals in a row, we can celebrate right away—we already have the money set aside. This also adds an extra layer of accountability for us! If we're going to set aside the money, we're expecting to achieve the goals!

Have some fun with this exercise. My hope is that your Bing-Goal Board opens your eyes to the *fun* behind your goals. It's *fun* to set some goals for you to achieve. It's *fun* to organize your goals with a Personal Priority List. It's *fun* to place your goals on a board and cross them off one by one. Most importantly, it's *fun* to know that you're making progress in your personal, professional and family life.

This Bing-Goal Board will be a constant reminder of both how far you've come and the exciting accomplishments that await you in your future. If you're climbing your Self-Discipline Tree, then you'll be able to look down and see how far you've climbed, as well as see how close you are to reaching the top of your tree!

Now that we've seen how to envision your path, set your goals and organize them successfully, there's one last thing we need to do in the Preparation Phase: cleanse ourselves of some negative influences. Let's get into it!

Chapter 4

CLEANSING

Like anyone else, I've had to deal with my fair share of negative influences in my life. In elementary school and middle school, "friends of mine" called me "stupid" for not getting straight A's like they did. As silly as it sounds, those constant lies convinced me that I was actually incapable of getting good grades in my classes. At some point I told myself, *"Well then, why should I even try?"*

Looking back, I only graduated middle school because I had teachers who legitimately cared about me. Sadly, that was no different in high school. My entire high school career was spent taking classes with kids in the grade below me. If I received even one less credit, I would've been held back a year. Why? Because I believed a lie from a bunch of elementary school kids for so many years.

My entire life, I've had two parents who loved me and have told me I was smarter than the grades I was getting. My family members, my coaches, my pastors and my closest friends all tried to give me just as much inspiration. Sadly, all of those words of encouragement fell on deaf ears because of my own self-doubt. I refused to believe that there was any substance to what they were saying.

So are those elementary kids—who didn't realize the effect of their words—to blame for my years of academic struggles? Absolutely not. But if *they* aren't responsible for my educational setback, who is? The answer—and this is going to sting for some of you—is *me*.

I'm the one that let myself believe those lies. *I'm* the one that chose not to rise to the challenge. It was me that stopped trying. It was me that didn't study for my tests out of fear that I'd get a "D" or an "F" after actually *trying* to study. I'm the one who thought it was "cool" to shrug off my academics and try to fit in with the cool kids at school instead—which didn't pan out, by the way. I thank the Lord every day that he gave me positive role models who refused to quit on me. I'm eternally grateful that I got a chance to redeem myself in college; some kids never get that opportunity.

Looking back on it now, here's the one thing that could've saved me—and eventually *did* save me—from all those years of falling short: I should've cleansed my life. I should've cut ties with the friends and connections that were fueling my self-doubt.

Would that have immediately solved my problems? No. I still had to fight through my self-loathing. However, cutting those relationships out of my life was the *first* step towards a better future; a future with more confidence and commitment to improving myself.

These days, the negative influences in our lives are plentiful. This could apply to the friends we hang out with, the apps we use, the social media platforms we scroll through, the family members that try to hold us back, the careers we prioritize at the expense of our relationships, the ex-girlfriend/ex-boyfriend that we refuse to close the door on—the list can go on and on.

In this chapter, I want to spend some time addressing the different things that can prevent us from accomplishing the goals we've set—*if we let them*. It's important to me that you realize how much *power* and *control* you actually have in accomplishing your goals. It all starts by identifying the negative influences in your life that will try to hold you back, then taking action to purge them from your path. I promise you, it *can* be done. Let's start with identifying some of the most common negative influences that we battle each day.

I. Negative Influences

Negative influences are an intriguing thing, when you think about them; we all struggle with them, but the types of toxic influences differ from person to person. There are some that are unique to your life and what you've gone through and others that are common amongst us all— are the ones we'll be covering in this header. As for the influences that are unique to you, we'll talk about a few helpful tactics I've found for cleansing *any* bad influence, regardless of what/who it is. For now, I'd like to focus on a few common influences that we all struggle with to some degree.

a. Time-Wasting Apps

Can I share with you one thing I've learned about time-wasting apps? Even if you *think* you don't struggle with time-wasting apps, you do. Each of us have specific time-wasting habits with certain apps, some more toxic than others.

While you might not struggle with scrolling endlessly through Facebook or Instagram, you might spend *way* too much time trying to beat your high score on Candy Crush. Even if you don't play games on your phone or have social media, you might spend too much time reading up on the latest sports news (I'm most guilty of this) or watching stocks rise and fall throughout the day.

Let me clarify that smartphone apps are not wicked. Does Candy Crush *force* you to play it three cumulative hours a day? No. Does YouTube lock your screen and constrain you to watch five videos in a row? Not that I'm aware of.

It isn't the app that's the negative influence, it's how you *use* it that determines whether or not it's a toxic element in your life. I'll mention a few methods for how to take back control of your smartphone tendencies later on in this chapter.

b. Self-Doubt

The story I shared in the beginning of this chapter is the perfect example of how self-doubt can wreck your life, if you let it. I let other people's harmful words fester into my own self-pity and insecurities. I allowed those words to dictate my progress and personal growth for far too long. I'd be willing to bet you have some self-doubt in your life as well; something that has been crippling your ascension in life.

I want to encourage you by saying this: whatever your self-doubt is telling you, *it isn't true*. Regardless of whatever excuses you've made for yourself or the past failures you've experienced, your self-doubt is nothing but a lie. As long as you're willing to put in the time and effort, there's *nothing* you can't do. It might take a few attempts to achieve the goal, but the victory will be even sweeter in the end.

The *most effective* way I've found to curb self-doubt is to build a strong, like-minded support system—we'll discuss how to build one in the third phase of this book. For now, it's important that you take the time to identify all of the self-doubt you're carrying in your life. As Sigmund Freud, an Australian neurologist, once said, "Being entirely honest with oneself is a good exercise".[1] Well put, Mr. Freud!

c. Toxic Relationships

Uh oh, reader. Did I just hit a little too close to home for you now? Don't wince away, I'll tread lightly.

There are four different types of relationships that we all have—family relationships, friendships, acquaintanceships and romantic relationships—and none of them are any less complicated than the other.[2]

Some of these relationships are pivotal to our growth—this could include mentors, role models, spouses, best friends, coworkers, etc.

Other relationships are toxic and inhibit your growth. I like to put these poisonous relationships into two categories: the ones you *can* get rid of and the ones you *can't*. I'd argue that any toxic relationship has the ability to be purged from your life unless they're a blood relative or you're legally tied to, such as the father/mother of your children (like an ex-spouse). Even then, you can do all you can to avoid coming into contact with them.

To put it simply, if people aren't interested in helping you work towards your goals, that relationship is of no use to you. By the way, if they talk bad about others behind *their* backs, you'd better believe they're doing the same to you. Move on from them! As one of the oldest adages tells us: "Who you hang around is who you become." If you don't want to become that person, don't hang around them.

d. Gossip

Doesn't it seem like the older you get, the more people gossip? Ignore the negative chatter around you, my friend. No matter how juicy the "news" is that you hear about your coworker or boss, it's not worth sinking your teeth into.

In fact, studies have shown that rumors and gossip can literally make you sick. Rumors can bring on physical and mental fatigue, increase your anxiety, and even lead to depression. Depending on the severity of the gossip, it can cause guilt, panic attacks, depression and even Post-Traumatic Stress Disorder (PTSD).[3] Is that something you'd wish on the person you're gossiping about? Of course not, so don't engage in it.

And don't think that you can spread gossip or engage in it and come out unscathed. If you take on the negative views of others, you also absorb their aggression, hostility and frustration towards that subject as well. These thoughts can easily warp your view of a situation, project or person, leading to poor judgment—which is a one-way ticket to making costly mistakes in your personal life, career and so forth.

My dad is good for several golden nuggets of wisdom, but his best one might be the one that *his* dad used to tell him about how to approach gossip: *"Don't believe anything you hear, and only half of what you see!"* If you hear hot gossip, don't engage in it. Even if you *think* you've witnessed something with your own eyes, there are always two sides to the story.

e. Your Personal Triggers

Personal triggers—also known as emotional triggers—are a topic, person, place or thing that brings on undesirable feelings; this can be anything from feeling ticked off after seeing your ex pop up on your social media, to feeling sad when you're forced to talk about a loved one who tragically passed away.

We all have triggers; however, it's how we handle them that's different. Some of us curl up in a ball when emotional triggers come our way. I prefer to do it the other way around—I take them head on.

The key to overcoming your personal/emotional triggers is knowing what they are in the first place. Once you've identified what your triggers are, you can either attempt to change them, purge them from your life or avoid them at all costs. Here are a few questions you can use to try and identify your personal triggers:

- *Is there someone that irks you every time they come around?*

- *What subjects make you flustered when you're forced to talk about them?*
- *What conversations do your loved ones bring up that frustrate you?*
- *Why do specific topics bother you? Are you insecure about that area of your life? Do you wish you had it for yourself?*
- *Is there someone in your life that you constantly compare yourself to?*

After asking these questions, be sure to point the focus back on you. I'd venture to guess that nine times out of 10, people don't intend to frustrate you. Look inside yourself and observe why that personal trigger exists. What can you do to relieve yourself of it? I've found that there's only one way to rid ourselves of our emotional triggers: you have to *own* them. Otherwise, they'll own you.

II. Cleansing Social Media Habits

That's right, people! We're getting down to the nitty-gritty, here. I want to preface this by saying that social media isn't evil. In fact, the concept of it is quite beautiful; it helps you build an online community where you can stay connected with anyone, no matter where they live. It isn't the app that's to blame for the hours you waste on it each day; it's your *habits* that are to blame. Is that harsh? Maybe. Is it true? Absolutely.

Here's the good part—you aren't alone in your struggles with social media. Out of the 50 surveys that I received from successful professionals in my network, 45 of them listed social media as something that they needed to cleanse from their lives; not "limit" from their lives. Not "tone down" in their lives. They said they realize the need to *cleanse* it. Remove it. Move on from it.

Why? Because they realize the same thing that we all do.

Social media has a tendency to negatively affect our lives. We start to play the comparison game with the picture-perfect lives that our connections seem to have. Spoiler alert: their lives aren't perfect either; they struggle with insecurities, too. Heck, they might even look at your photos and think that *you* have the perfect life. How's *that* for a mind-bender? We'll talk about how to overcome the comparison game in a later chapter, don't you worry!

The truth is that the social media platforms you use (Facebook, Instagram, Twitter, etc.) don't control the negativity that fills your head—you do. Take ownership of that; find reassurance in that. If you can control the negativity that comes from how you use social media, then you can either change it or get rid of it.

One of the biggest reasons that social media can be seen as a time-waster is because of the tendency we have to "fall down the rabbit hole." You know, the rabbit hole that suddenly turns "checking my updates" into scrolling for 30 minutes nonstop—*that* rabbit hole.

Do you know where that phrase originally comes from? It's a reference to the story of *Alice in Wonderland*. Much like the situation she found herself in, going down the rabbit hole on your smartphone can bring you to a situation you wouldn't otherwise be in (like checking your ex-boyfriend's latest photos at 2 a.m. or watching "gym fails" on YouTube for two consecutive hours).

I can relate to that second one!

Admittedly, my biggest weakness was watching sports highlights on YouTube. If it were up to me, I would spend my entire day watching the career highlights of every one of my favorite all-time athletes. Then I'd inevitably look at the time and roll my eyes at myself.

I'm not alone. Studies show that even those of us that are tame in our social media use can potentially spend up to 2.5 hours a day on various platforms.[4] That means that most of us spend *at least* 2.5 hours each day doing something that hinders us from our goals; that's 17.5 hours a week, 75 hours each month and 912.5 hours each *year* that you can't get back! Am I driving the point home, yet? Social media or otherwise, how can we take back control of these time-wasting apps? I have two exercises for you to try.

III. Take Back Control of Your Apps

Before I get to the two exercises, I want to challenge you with this thought: one day, you're going to be sitting in a chair (I'm visualizing a rocking chair) hanging out with your grandkids. If you know anything about young children, you know that they can ask some pretty *hard-hitting* questions without any remorse; they have no shame. What if one of your grandchildren asks you why you didn't get your dream job in life? What if they ask you why you never pursued your dream career? Do you really want to tell them that you were too busy reading social media posts and playing phone games?

Again, I want to stress that social media is beautiful in moderation. However, if you can't control the grasp it has on your life, you'll waste *many* hours that you could've been towards your goals; I know this because I've *lived* it.

Do you want to know the true secret to successful self-discipline? Here it is: **stick to what works and get rid of what distracts you**. Read that last sentence one more time. Memorize it. Apply it.

Now then, let's talk about how you can take back control of time-wasting apps. As previously mentioned, I have two different exercises for you; I call them the Zero-Notification Exercise and the Purge-and-Reassess Exercise. You can probably guess what they entail by the directness of their names, but I'll explain them both in greater detail.

Start with the Zero-Notification Exercise. Give it one month to see if it helps you retain control of your smartphone usage. If in one month you don't notice any improvements, then it's time to try the Purge-and-Reassess Exercise. Let's dive into both right now.

Exercise #1: Zero-Notifications

This is a tremendous exercise for those of you who recognize a need to cut out the noise, but don't necessarily need to eradicate social media from your life; it can also help those of your that click on certain apps as soon as you open your phone out of habit—you know who you are.

Here's the exercise: go into your smartphone's settings and simply turn off all push notifications from all the apps that you deem as time-wasters. By doing this, you'll have less distractions throughout your day. Most of us get a push notification that "Sandy posted for the first time in a while" and, without thinking, drop what we're doing because our curiosity gets the best of us. With those push notifications turned off, you won't feel a sense of urgency to constantly check your phone.

Two things I want to add before moving on to the second exercise. First, if the app adds zero value to your life (such as a game you play *way* too often), it should be deleted. Turning off the push notifications won't stop the habit you have of opening the game every 15 minutes to play. If you delete the app, you aren't likely to go through the hassle of ever re-downloading it.

Second, don't turn off the push notifications to the apps you need in your life. For example, I keep push notifications on for my banking app, Bible app, Calendar, E-mail, etc. I don't want you blaming me for not remembering to pay your bills next month!

Evaluate yourself each week. Your phone might also update you on whether your phone activity was up or down from the previous week. If after four weeks you aren't seeing improvements, it's time to move on to the Purge-and-Reassess exercise.

Exercise #2: Purge-and-Reassess

Granted, this exercise is much more extreme. But as the old saying goes, sometimes "Desperate times call for desperate measures!" I recommend the Purge-and-Reassess Exercise if you think your apps are either wasting your time or poisoning your mind, but you can't pinpoint which ones are causing the issues.

Here's what to do: start by deleting all of your extracurricular apps from your phone, including social media, sports apps, entertainment, games, streaming services—the works!

Go one entire week without re-downloading any of them; you'll be shocked at the amount of focus and time that this puts back into your day. Removing those apps can also reduce your stress levels and help you keep a positive mindset; your spouse, coworkers and managers will *definitely* notice a change.

Each week after, re-download one app each week, starting with the ones that you don't think are causing you any issues. Once you find yourself falling back into a habit of procrastination and increased stress, you've found the primary apps that are at fault. Once you figure out those apps, delete them for good!

If I'm being honest with you, reader, this is the exercise *I* had to use. I realized my phone was distracting me, but I couldn't figure out why; I wasn't scrolling through social media; I'm not a big fan of texting; I haven't downloaded a game on my phone in years. Still, I could *not* figure out what was causing me to procrastinate all day.

So I decided to try this Purge-and-Reassess exercise for myself. Long story short, I eventually figured out that it was a sports app that was my primary distraction. Almost immediately after I re-downloaded it, my productivity plummeted. Every time I got an update from that app, I checked it. I'd scroll through its news feed endlessly. Once my eyes were opened to this fact, it all made perfect sense.

As much as it pained me to do, I deleted the app and haven't re-downloaded it since; that was half a year ago at the time of me writing this. Looking back, *I'm so glad I did*. Don't get me wrong, I still check up on the latest sports news in my free time; but since I don't have that sports app anymore, I've found a way to get all my sports news at once rather than mindlessly checking it every 20 minutes.

I guarantee you that one of these two exercises will provide you with clarity. They will help you free your life from the needless distractions that are preventing you from accomplishing the goals you set in Chapter 2. Heck, if you feel like the Zero-Notification exercise won't resolve your issue, then start the Purge-and-Reassess exercise from the get-go. Do whatever it takes to take back control of your smartphone and your time, my friend.

IV. Temptation

Temptation comes to us in many forms on a daily basis; there's the temptation to quit, run, spend, lust, slack off, doubt, veer away from our purpose and many more. Those are just cracking the surface.

The good news? By implementing the steps in Chapters 1 through 4 thus far, you've already purged a bulk of those temptations from your life. By creating a vision, you've eliminated the desire to run from your situation. In creating goals and cleansing your life, you've eliminated the temptation to slack off. There are some temptations on that list that I'm not qualified to talk about, though. Not to get on a soapbox here, but if you struggle with things like lust, spending or coveting, I'd recommend you open another book: The Bible!

For *this* book, I want to focus on the three forms of temptation that I think hinder us from our goals the most—the temptation to quit, doubt or pursue other goals. Let's dive into each one!

a. The Temptation to Quit

We've all been through this temptation enough. For every goal that you work toward, there will always come a time where you feel the urge to give up. I'd venture to say that you'll face this more than once with each goal you go after, but why?

Because sometimes life smacks us in the face.

Life can create a scenario where it seems like your goals are either too high of a mountain to climb or not worth the effort. Here's what I think: if we've put in the work to set the goal and set ourselves up for success (which we've done in Phase One), then it's *never* too high of a mountain and it's *always* worth overcoming.

Here's the real reason I think we get the urge to quit: we lose our vision for success. Think about it… when you first set a goal, you can envision yourself achieving that goal. For example, with my goal of writing this book, I can envision holding it my hands. But when that vision starts to feel too distant, that's when we're tempted to quit.

As cheesy as it sounds, my go-to move when I want to quit is writing down and reading aloud inspirational quotes from successful people. How about this one from the late author, James A. Michener, that reads "Character consists of what you do on the third and fourth tries." Or Vince Lombardi's famous quote of "Winners never quit, and quitters never win." Need one more? Let's use Nelson Mandela's catchphrase, "It always seems impossible until it's done."[5]

The point is, any goal that you've set out for is possible, but it might not always be easy. Be ready for failure. Rub some dirt on it and keep climbing that tree! Successful self-discipline is conjured up inside; only you have the power to tell yourself "No, self. I'm not quitting on this goal!"

b. The Temptation to Doubt

Whenever our vision or end result gets blurry, there's also another form of temptation that occurs; you start to doubt yourself. You start to think *"Maybe I'm not capable of achieving this after all."*

Maybe you'll find it encouraging to know that I've been there too. In fact, I've put off writing this book for *years* because of that doubt inside. Doubt will always creep inside, if you let it. It's like a cockroach that makes its way inside a home—it can only get inside if there's an opening. Once it's inside, it can spread like wildfire. There's only one option after you see one inside: exterminate it!

There are three tips I have for overcoming self-doubt when it shows its ugly face.

First, take a look at your past achievements, at how far you've come in your life. Think of all the goals you've accomplished, regardless of whether they're related to your current goals or not. Remember, you had obstacles with those goals, too. You overcame them then, and you'll overcome any setbacks in the future as well!

Second, surround yourself with the right support network. We'll talk about this extensively in our Accountability Chapter, but here's the gist: you have to find a support system that's like-minded—those that are working hard towards their own goals, rather than weighing you down. If you surround yourself with lazy, negative people, you'll have no one to help you out of your rut.

Third, eliminate doubt through action. Tell your own self-doubt that you're going to prove it wrong by working toward your goal. I promise you, that self-doubt will subside through hard work. As you gain momentum and accomplish little checkpoints toward your goal, you'll have proven to yourself that the self-doubt was wrong all along.

c. Temptation to Pursue Other Goals

I could ask 10 people what their biggest temptation is when working towards their long-term goals, and I doubt any of them would mention the temptation to pursue other goals; it's a very real thing! I might be the poster child for this temptation.

I have an entrepreneurial spirit inside me; a quiet confidence that I can achieve anything I can put my mind to—which is a blessing and a curse. It's a blessing because it gives me confidence in anything I do. It's a curse because it makes me believe that there's no such thing as a bad idea. In fact, while I'm working towards writing this book—which is taking most of my time—I'm also thinking of two separate business ventures that are intriguing to me. You see my dilemma.

That's the struggle with self-discipline, isn't it? There will always be new opportunities that present themselves, but are those opportunities worth giving up your current long-term goals? It depends on the situation, but a majority of the time, the answer is no.

There's a reason you began down this journey. Again, whenever the end goal seems too far away, we start to look east or west instead of keeping our eyes to the north. Are you following me?

One of my buddies is currently working on acquiring his Ph.D. in Business Administration with a Concentration in Accounting. As you might imagine, it takes up the bulk of his time. I love the way he put it when he told me, "Without being disciplined, I would be curious of many different career opportunities and not focused on the one I'm called to do. Self-discipline allows me to have a healthy level of curiosity, while not losing sight of the goal I am working towards."

In other words, focus on the goals you feel called to. This is easy for me because of my faith. I know exactly which goals God calls me to, and which ones he's leaving for others to pursue. If you ever need guidance on determining which goals you're called to do, I'm here to help. Visit my website, zachmathewswriting.com, and we'll find your path together.

V. Cleansing by Replacing

One final thought before we move on to the next phase of our Self-Discipline Tree. What if you were to replace your bad habits with good ones? I realize that's an oversimplification, but hear me out.

If a psychological habit loop always includes a cue, a routine and a reward (as the great Charles Duhigg pointed out in *The Power of Habit),* then what would happen if we replaced the bad routine with a good routine?

For example, instead of picking up your phone and scrolling endlessly (the bad routine) whenever you get bored (the cue), why not pick up a book?

Instead of watching YouTube videos (the bad routine) while you're on the elliptical or treadmill at the gym (the cue), why not turn on an audiobook or podcast that applies to your long-term goals?

Trust me, this takes time to change, but it can be done! Don't get discouraged when it doesn't come naturally. You've been scrolling on your phone for years—it's ingrained in your brain. Your brain isn't just going to dump that habit after you pick up a book one time, no matter how riveting the book might be—like this book right here!

Here's my claim: I'll bet that you can cleanse any negative or time-wasting habit you have with a good one by simply altering the routine. In fact, I'll bet that once you change the routine, you'll witness an even *greater* reward. I think we can all agree you'll feel better after running a mile when you're bored than playing mini golf on your phone when you're bored.

Give it a try. Start by trying to change the routine of *one* bad habit you have. I promise you, if you can take back control of one bad routine, your long-term goals are that much closer. The choice is yours—stay stagnant with the habits that inhibit you from achieving your dreams or change them and watch success become a reality.

As the great Greek philosopher Aristotle once said, "We are what we repeatedly do. Excellence, then, is not an action, but a habit."[6] Speaking of *act*... Let's jump into Phase 2: the Production Phase, to learn how to put our newfound goals into act-*ion*!

PHASE 2:

PRODUCTION

CHAPTER 5

EXERCISE

There's no denying it—there is a direct correlation between fitness and successful self-discipline. Those that make time for the gym, court, field, etc. are the same ones that are more likely to hit their long-term goals.

Studies have shown that nearly 80-percent of U.S. adults and children aren't getting the adequate amount of exercise they need to maintain their optimal health.[1]

Studies have also shown that 92-percent of people never achieve the goals that they set out to hit. Coincidence?[2] I think not.

Here's the weird part: we all *know* the importance of exercise. We know that it's in our best interests to work out and get outside for no fewer than 20 minutes a day. We realize that our nutrition can be vastly improved—which is covered in our next chapter, by the way—but we still order the #4 with large fries and a large soda. Why? Because it's a *habit*. Let me explain.

Growing up, my little sister and I were always involved in sports. No matter what time of year it was, we always had practices, games, meets and matches after school. At the time, my mom was going back to school to be a nurse and my dad had a demanding career. Both of them had to balance getting us to church, school and sports on time.

They cooked home meals for us as often as they could, but there were nights where getting fast food made more sense from a timing/schedule standpoint. I can recall several instances where we ate dinner on the drive from basketball practice to Wednesday night church service.

Because I was raised on it, I've always loved fast food. In fact, I'd love nothing more than to run to Taco Bell right now, order three loaded beef grillers, two soft tacos, cinnamon twists and a large Mountain Dew Baja Blast—but I refrain.

A while ago, I realized fast food was a *crutch* for me, so I cut it out of my life. Some people never come to that realization; they grab fast food because it's convenient instead of cooking a healthier meal at home; they reach for the remote instead of a dumbbell; rather than going on a run, they go on a binge-watching spree every night without consciously thinking about it.

Can I let you in on a secret? Those habits are—whether you like it or not—an exact representation of your self-discipline.

If you choose to lay around instead of exerting energy to improve your health by working out, I'd be willing to bet you have the same discipline when it comes to working towards your goals. You set the goals, but you tell yourself, *"Eh, I'll do it later…"*

Here's the good news: even if you *do* currently push aside your exercise goals, you can correct your habits!

Exercise is a keystone habit. Remember Charles Duhigg, author of *The Power of Habit*? He describes keystone habits as "small changes or habits that people introduce into their routines that unintentionally carry over into other aspects of their lives."[3]

In other words—if you stop making excuses for skipping your workouts, you'll stop making excuses for not working towards your goals. If you take the time to organize your daily workouts, you'll take the time to organize your personal and professional life.

In this chapter, I'm going to give you some tips on how to find an exercise routine that you'll stick to. Just to clarify, you won't find any workout plans, here—merely ways to stick to an exercise plan that you choose, and get the right mindset to attack your exercise goals. Let's get into it!

I. Find the "Why" Behind the Workout

Why do most of our workout plans never pan out? Why does it seem like we quit every workout routine before we even start to see the results? I would venture to say that a bulk of us are failing those plans from the get-go.

Hear me out. Many of us fall for the latest fitness fad. We come across a program that our friends/relatives have seen success with—maybe they've lost a significant amount of weight with it or they gained some muscle definition from it. Naturally, we want that for ourselves. We purchase the workout plan without even reading into the different phases. How do you think that's going to pan out? For some reason, I'm envisioning an image of that workout plan getting lost between the seats in your car. Maybe I'm off.

I used to be guilty of this myself. As a college athlete, I must've tried at least a dozen different 12-week workout plans that I found online—I won't say where. I'd be willing to bet that I averaged quitting them somewhere between the fourth to fifth week. Why? Because I didn't actually *understand* the workout.

I'll give myself a little credit, here. Even though I'd quit the workout plan, I'd still go to the gym three to four times a week—granted, some of those days I was just going through the motions.

My senior year, I found a workout plan that I actually stuck with—I followed it to a "T." After the 12 weeks were over, I was in the best shape of my life! Wanting the progress to continue, I started the plan all over again, but *this* time, one of my freshman teammates did it with me.

It was a power-building workout plan, which meant we would focus on doing a high number of sets, low repetitions and add the weight after each set. One day, while we were doing deadlifts, my teammate asked me, "Why do we raise the amount of the weight instead of raising the number of reps that we do?" It was a great question... I didn't have an answer for him.

That's when it occurred to me—we have to know the *why* behind the workout. If you're going to stick with a workout plan, you have to find one that you truly believe in. The best way to find a plan that you trust is by understanding the method behind their madness. Why are they having you perform three sets instead of four? Why do they separate the workouts into chest day, leg day, shoulder day and arm day? Why is it important that you follow them in that specific order? Uh oh, they're starting to have you perform exercises in groups of two (aka supersets) in the next phase...why?

If a workout plan *doesn't* explain itself, it isn't worth your time. I'm not one to spend big money on workout plans, but I'd gladly pay $100 for a workout routine that explains the thought process behind it rather than pay $10 for one that doesn't.

One last thought before we move on to the next point; I've found that I stick with the workout plans from people I trust. I'm not talking about getting a workout plan from your brother; I mean finding a trustworthy expert—this can be a professional trainer, a social influencer or that guy from the gym whose biceps are bigger than the size of your head. If you know the person well enough and see them applying the workout to their own routine, you're more likely to stick with it *and* see the results you want.

II. Find a Practical Workout Plan

There aren't many of us that can shift our entire day around a workout routine; as important as working out is, we have higher priorities like making it to work on time, taking the kids to school and preparing dinner for the family, to name a few.

I know how it goes. Whenever you first tell yourself, *"I'm going to get back in shape!"* you're riding a high; you're ready to commit to anything and everything that the workout plan has for you—even if that means spending two hours a night at the gym or doing exercises you wouldn't normally do.

But eventually, that high starts to fade. You find yourself mentally drained from a long day at work and don't have the energy to work out that night. The exercises start to get tiresome. The reps start to become more, well, *repetitive.*

The good news is that I know *exactly* what's causing this issue time and time again. There are two things, actually.

First, you aren't performing a workout that fits your preferred workout method. There are many different workout methods out there: interval training, weight training, flexibility training, plyometric training, cardiovascular training and so on. It's important to find one *that makes sense to you.* If you don't like running, then cardiovascular training probably shouldn't be your top form of exercise. With that said, we all need to suck it up and do a bit of cardio once in a while! It's the best way to build up endurance and lose body weight, among many other great benefits. Find a training method that you like, and then find a workout plan that supports it.

Second, the workout you've chosen *hinders* your daily schedule, when it should be *complimenting* it. I'll give you an example. I really enjoy weightlifting; it challenges me, it motivates me and I feel *really* good about myself after doing it. *But,* I also love playing sports. I've been an athlete my whole life. These days, I get my sports fix through activities like playing golf, slow-pitched softball, lacrosse, basketball, and more—any activity with a ball involved will do.

My weightlifting workouts are used to compliment the sports that I play. Am I saying that you all have to follow my example? Absolutely not. It's just a balance I've found that keeps me active, happy and looking forward to my workouts the next day. I want you to know what that's like as well, if you don't already.

My advice is to find a workout plan that's practical to your life. In time, it will become a part of your day that you look forward to, not dread.

III. Track Your Results

Okay, reader. I'm going to get on my soapbox for just a moment. It pains me to see people who take the time out of their day to drive to the gym and work out, but don't track their results; maybe they think they'll remember the weight they did from last week, but that's a tall order. I can't even remember what I had for breakfast yesterday. There's no way I'd remember the reps or weight that I lifted last week if I didn't track it.

Tracking your results, no matter what training method you perform, will provide you with accountability; it can make help your goals a reality. It provides you with all the motivation you need to go back and work out the next day as you see and experience gradual growth. You'll be more consistent, too.

This is just one more example of why exercise is a keystone habit. If you track your workout results, you'll start tracking the results of your personal goals and professional goals as well.

So how should you track your results? Some workout plans will make it easy on you. They might have a blank space for you to enter in the information in a workbook.

For those of you that don't have that luxury, here's what I recommend you track: the duration of your workout (start to finish), the exercises you performed, the number of reps and sets you did and the weight you lifted.

Also, if you have a smartwatch that keeps track of the calories you burned, be sure to write that down! Keep in mind, some of these might not apply to the training method that you use.

Just to provide a little more clarity, I'll give you an example from one of my own workouts!

Bench Press - 6 sets - 135x15, 155x12, 185x10, 205x8, 225x6, 225x6

I realize that might look like gibberish to you, so I'll elaborate. First, we have the exercise, which in this case is "Bench Press"—pretty self-explanatory. Next, we have the number of sets I performed, which was six sets. Again, pretty self-explanatory. Just to the right of that is detailed information on the weight and sets that I did. For example, the "135x15" means that I lifted 135 pounds for 15 reps, "225x6" means I benched 225 pounds for 6 reps, etc. Don't judge me if you can lift more—I'm a work in progress!

You don't have to keep track of your workouts the way I do; all that matters is that you're recording your progress and that it makes sense to you. Also, be sure to actually write it down. You can use a pen and journal if you'd like, but I just use the Notes app on my phone.

Tracking your workouts will give you more power—pun intended. It will give you all the inspiration you need to come back and try to beat your performance from last week's chest day, arm day, leg day, etc.

IV. Have the Right Outlook

At this point, two words come to mind: your outlook and your mindset. You need to have the right outlook on your workouts because it encourages you to look at the big picture i.e. what you're doing this for.

Having the right mindset, in my opinion, is more helpful for getting yourself to the gym and taking the workout seriously. We all have days where we go through the motions, but if you have the right *mindset* on the workout, you'll see better results.

So how do you get to this point? You get there by viewing your workout as a *reward,* not a chore; it's something you *get* to do, not something that you *have* to do. It's a chance to unplug from your busy, hectic day and go improve yourself. Why would we ever view that as a nuisance?

I understand being tired. I understand the letdown of not seeing the results that you want right away. But here's some food for thought: exercising boosts your energy and your mood. In a way, the best medicine for feeling tired or disappointed is to work out. Trippy, right?

There'll be times where you feel like you're in a rut. You might go through *weeks* of fighting yourself to get to the gym. I've felt that, too. Many times!

Whenever I find myself in a funk with my workouts and lack the desire to go, I use something that I call "the power of new." I'm not a materialistic person at all, but whenever I get something new for my workouts, I get revitalized; I start looking forward to the gym all over again! The "new" could be things like starting a new workout plan, buying new shoes or getting a new shirt and so on—it gives me a second wind.

That's a lesson you can use in any area of your life. Are you getting tired of working towards your career goals? Buy a new suit. Tired of taking the same commute to work? Find a new podcast to listen to. Switch up the routine. Throw yourself a curveball. You'll be surprised at the difference it makes!

V. Establish Your Workout Goals

I must sound like a broken record at this point, right? Here I go again talking about setting goals for yourself! But let me ask you this—what is the primary goal you have for your current workout? If you can't answer that question right away, you need to reassess things.

Workout goals are essential. Just like we went over in our Goal-Setting Chapter, I'm a big proponent of setting big goals, with small goals that feed into them. The small goals serve as a checkpoint, in a way.

Those of you that work out without goals are getting in your own way. Try to imagine a contractor starting construction on a home without a blueprint. Would you recommend someone start a small business without a business plan? You get the point.

As I've already mentioned in this chapter, I've played sports my entire life. Ever since I can remember, I was playing on a team of some kind, no matter the time of year; it gave me something to look forward to. It was merely a way for me to burn off the energy that I—being a hyperactive kid—had pent up inside. Sports were merely the means to an end to me for a long time. Sadly, that was partially my mindset in high school as well.

That all changed when I became a college athlete. For the first time in my life, I understood the importance of practice. I knew *exactly* why I was lifting weights and running sprints. Did I enjoy running suicides the length of the field until our head coach got tired of blowing the whistle? Not at all. But I knew the "why" behind it. I knew that everything we were doing was to compete for a conference championship.

All of a sudden, that goal of working towards a championship was ripped out from under me when I graduated. Suddenly, there wasn't a coach to blow a whistle at me anymore. My teammates weren't there to push me (and I them). Not to mention that my strength and conditioning didn't directly correlate to my goals in life. It's not like my boss was going to give me a manager position because of how many times I could deadlift 300 pounds (although I wish it worked that way).

Instead, I had to find new goals to keep myself in the gym. The best solution I've found is to have your primary workout goal be within reach, by a certain date. For example, losing weight before your wedding or bulking up before a beach vacation with your friends/family next summer. That last one is my current primary goal, by the way!

Once you have your primary workout goal in place, use that to fuel your smaller workout goals—goals that will slowly help you chip away at the big one. For example, I currently have a goal to perform five muscle ups in a row. If you don't know what that is, look it up on YouTube—it's hard to explain. I've only ever done two in a row, and they were iffy at best—again, don't laugh at me.

Make your workout goals individualistic to you. They'll change with time. Once you knock those out of the park, you can find new standards for improving your workouts and fitness routine! Setting goals to see progress… isn't that the goal of exercise in the first place?

VI. Chip Away at Your Fitness Goals

So far in this chapter, we've learned how to find the "why" behind our workout, how to find a practical workout plan, how to track our results, how to have the right outlook on our exercise routines and how to establish clear goals (both big and small).

Checking off each of these one by one will help you see improved results and establish habits in the gym that will work their way into your professional, personal and family habits. However, I want to make this abundantly clear—it won't make your fitness goals any easier; that's not how this works. If your exercises aren't pushing you to your limits each day—and therefore aren't helping you better yourself—then they are a complete waste of your time.

One of my biggest pet peeves is hearing people talk about how they "embraced the grind" while building their startup business, losing a significant amount of weight or any other substantial goal. I think that term—"the grind"—is an oversimplification to the hard work and dedication it takes to succeed at anything in life.

If getting a six-pack was truly as easy as "embracing the grind," wouldn't more people succeed at it?

Here's where I'm going with this: changing your current trend of picking up a workout routine and dropping it halfway through is going to be difficult. Whether you like it or not, that is a *habit* that you've established. To eradicate that habit from your life, you'll have to replace it with a new habit. Habits take a *long* time to correct. It takes months for a new behavior to become automatic.

Rather than trying to sugarcoat how difficult it is to stick with a workout by telling you to "embrace the grind," I'll say it another way. I want you to *chip away* at that workout. I want you to approach every day as a new day to push yourself to new limits—because that's *exactly* what it is.

You know what I love most about workout plans? While the workout routines you follow and the one I follow might be vastly different, we're both working towards the same goal: to get better. To look better. To *feel* better.

Working towards that goal through exercise and activity unlocks something in us that can't be duplicated anywhere else in life. Once you've unlocked the passion and discipline to push yourself in your workouts each day, you can unlock that passion anywhere else in your life. I *truly* believe that.

It's no coincidence that countless professional athletes have gone on to be successful businessmen and businesswomen after their careers were over—Magic Johnson, Shaq and James Clear—to name a few. It goes beyond the platform they built during their athletic career. They allocate the tenacity, passion and competitive drive they unlocked as an athlete towards their respective businesses.

I think Kobe Bryant described this unlocked potential best. It's what he referred to as the infamous "Mamba Mentality." In his book, *The Mamba Mentality,* he described the way he approached everything in life. I'm not doing it justice, here, but essentially it was his mindset to attack everything in his life with passion and drive. He used that passion and drive to outwork everyone else. As he once said himself, "Hard work outweighs talent every time."[4]

For me personally, I can't go to sleep at night knowing I underperformed or gave something less than my all. Ask my wife, it keeps me awake at night.

I'd venture to guess that a lot of you reading this are the same way. Some of you may have noticed that you've been coasting through your daily life the past few weeks, months or even years. I've been there before, too—we all have!

For me, workouts are the best way to ensure I keep that competitive and hard-working mindset. In fact, I've noticed that the days I struggle with this the most is on "rest days"— the days I intentionally take off from the gym to recover.

If you're going to climb your Self-Discipline Tree and achieve your goals, you need to get stronger—and I don't mean that literally.

Both exercising and focusing on your nutrition (the next chapter) are keystone habits you *have* to nail down; if you do, I promise you'll maximize each day and keep your eyes on the prize. Learning the self-discipline it takes to monitor and correct these two aspects of life will naturally work their way into other areas of your life. Now that we've seen how exercise plays a role in successful self-discipline, let's take a gander at how nutrition applies to it as well!

CHAPTER 6

NUTRITION

I'd venture to guess that a majority of you made some sort of personal fitness goal for yourselves back in the Goal-Setting Chapter—that's great! We should all strive to get in better shape and find a sustainable way to promote a healthy lifestyle. Notice that I wrote the word *sustainable.*

We've all wanted six-pack abs at one point or another in our lives, but is it sustainable? You might be surprised to find that the answer is *yes*; however, you'll have to make some adjustments in your life to keep your body fat percentage low enough to make those abs visible.

Some of you have no interest in altering your workout and nutrition enough to keep a ripped physique—that's perfectly fine, too! I'm a *huge* advocate for finding a physique that you're most comfortable with and confident in. Whatever weight, form, shape, or body mass index that takes, I'm game!

Thanks to the techniques you've learned in this book up to this point, you're ready to hit fitness goals that you never thought possible; but the route to hitting those goals might be *vastly* different from what you expected.

Most people assume that in order to lose weight and get your ideal physique, you have to work out non-stop; that couldn't be further from the truth. It's true that exercise is an important component to losing weight, building muscle, or whatever fitness goals you have; however, your *nutrition* is even more important.

As a matter of fact, experts go so far as to say that weight loss is 80-percent based on your nutrition and only 20-percent based on your workouts.[1] Even so, your workouts are still incredibly important—don't give them up!

In this chapter, you won't find any meal recommendations, recipes, or quick ways to lose the weight—or gain the muscle—that you might have been hoping for.

Instead, I want this chapter to shine a light on nutrition and why it's so important for establishing self-discipline in your *entire* life. I promise you this: if you're able to take control of your nutrition, you'll gain an advantage in life.

One shocking statistic reveals that over 97-percent of dieters end up regaining all the weight that they lost—and more—within three years.[2] You see what I mean about finding a *sustainable* fitness plan? Slow and steady wins the race. It's up to us to establish better, cleaner nutritional habits. If you can pull this off—and you can!—then you'll be a foot in front of 97-percent of health-conscious people.

If you're going to climb your Self-Discipline Tree, then you need to fuel up the right way with better eating habits. Let's start by focusing on what a diet *really* is and why it doesn't require as exhaustive an effort as you'd think.

I. The True Definition of "Diet"

Most of us hear the word *diet* and immediately think back to some phony "get shredded quick" meal plan that we once tried.

If I'm being honest, "diet" is another word that I cringe at; it is used *way* too much in society these days—even companies who make sugar-loaded, carbonated beverages can literally put the word "diet" in their name. It's situations like that which have given the word a negative connotation.

The Oxford Language dictionary defines a diet as "the kinds of food that a person, animal or community habitually eats." Did you catch that last part? "Habit." There's that word again!

I'm not one of them, but when true nutrition experts are telling you to take back control of your nutrition, they aren't telling you to pick up the latest diet fad in the industry. If those work for you, then that's great! But are they sustainable?

Sustainability *has* to be the determining factor in the diet you develop for yourself. But where should you begin?

Of all the nutritional information I've read/heard in my life, I love how Darin Olien puts it in his book, *SuperLife*, the best. He uses the book to teach the five "life forces" of maximizing our body's natural potential. Can you guess what the first of the five life forces is? That's right, quality nutrition.

He states that, when it comes to quality nutrition, we should focus on eating whole foods (vegetables, fruits, nuts, legumes, seeds, etc.)—foods that are fresh, raw and clean, which ultimately enhances our variety.[3] I won't give anymore of the book away, but if you're interested in getting more into the science behind your body's natural health, I highly recommend that you read *SuperLife*.

What's the takeaway, here? It's that eating habits, or a healthy diet, aren't as impossible as some would believe them to be. My recommendation? Learn all that you can about the eating habits of those who maintain a physique they're comfortable and happy with. Research the science behind what you eat. Start with the basics like learning about things such as your Total Daily Energy Expenditure (TDEE), caloric intakes, macro-nutrients and so on.

If there's one thing I've learned about nutrition, it's that experience is often the best teacher. Try different whole foods, mix in more vegetables, cut the junk food out of your life and stop drinking soda. I'm speaking from experience, people! If you work on cutting out the unhealthy habits in your nutrition, you'll be more than halfway to accomplishing your fitness goals already!

II. The Connection Between Nutrition and Self-Discipline

You can probably see a bit of the correlation between nutrition and successful self-discipline; not eating the last brownie; not going back for second portions of pasta; reaching for a protein shake instead of a handful of Sour Patch Kids. Am I the only one?

However, the connection between the two goes *much* further than that. One of my mentors once told me that, "Your investment in your personal health is a direct indication of your ability to self-discipline yourself." How's *that* for a proverb?

Let me phrase it another way. The attention and discipline you use toward your nutrition and personal health is an *exact* representation of your ability to control yourself. *Let that sink in.*

If you can't say no to sugary sweets and desserts in your diet, then you can't say no to quick moments of pleasure, even if they're at the expense of your long-term goals.

If you can't follow a structured meal plan with your nutrition or workouts, then you can't follow any concrete plans you make to accomplish your life goals.

If you aren't able to learn more about the food you should eat and how to balance out your plate each meal, and then apply it, you probably refuse to do the same with your career goals. You get the idea.

Your nutrition is the keystone habit of all keystone habits. If you can break the negative habits you have in your eating, then breaking any other negative habits in your life will seem minuscule in comparison; *that* should be reassuring for all of us.

If you want to kick-start a new life for yourself, start with changing your diet for the better.

I'm not qualified to give you specifics on how to go about doing that, but here are a few places to start.

- Throw out all the junk food inside your pantry.
- Stop drinking soda.
- Eat vegetables with every meal.

We all know this stuff, yet we fail to do it anyways. Why? Because that junk food and soda has become a habit; it gives us a brief moment of satisfaction—*very* brief, I might add.

We talked about Charles Duhigg's Habit Loop Model in a previous chapter: Cue, Routine and Reward. This model is the cadence for developing every habit since the dawn of time. We often go for the routines that give us a brief "reward"—such as eating a bag of chips—when a much more fulfilling reward awaits us if we choose a healthier routine.

I'm not claiming to be a saint here, folks; I struggle with this kind of stuff all the time. About a decade ago, I stopped drinking soda completely. A few years after that, I stopped going to fast food restaurants for my meals. My point is that I've struggled with them all, but I haven't overcome them all—not yet at least!

Nutrition is such a pivotal habit that fixing it for the better, even making a *tiny* tweak to it, can kick-start other healthier habits—even ones that have *nothing* to do with nutrition. If you stop using coffee as a crutch for energy, you'll start to become more consistent in your job performance—I'm not kidding!

A few years ago, I noticed that I was getting to work with a groggy feeling every morning; I'd literally sit at my desk and scroll the internet for 30 minutes before doing anything productive.

I traced back my morning routine to find out what I was doing wrong. Long story short, I found out that my breakfast was the culprit. Instead of giving me the energy I needed, it was basically putting me into a "food coma" every morning; I *had* to make an adjustment.

That's when I gave intermittent fasting a try for the first time. I started waiting until noon every day before consuming any food or beverage besides water—and black coffee (which is allowed). Once noon hit, I had eight hours to consume all of my calories for the day. Once 8 p.m. came around, that was it and I couldn't consume anything else until noon the next day.

Sounds brutal, right? That's what I thought at first too. In fact, I remember trying it out for the first time and fully expecting to give it up in less than a week, tops.

Instead, I came across a newfound freedom! Instead of letting my stomach dictate my schedule, *I* set the terms. This allowed me to take back control of my eating habits. It also made it easier for me to track my caloric intake whenever I was trying to bulk or cut—I only had to track calories for one-third of the day.

This isn't a subtle plug for intermittent fasting. I'm not recommending that you have to integrate it into your life. If you *are* going to try it, be sure to consult with your physician first; it isn't right for everyone.

My point here is that learning and trying different things with your nutrition can have a *huge* impact on the rest of your life; you just have to be willing to give them a shot.

III. Understanding Your Eating Habits

Let's get down to the nitty-gritty: why do we eat the way we do? Why have our eating habits become so subconscious that we're able to grab a handful of chips (or more) without even thinking about it?

For many of us, these habits started a *long* time ago—maybe with an innocent visit to the local ice cream stop—but have now become as familiar to us as the back of our hand.

The problem is that those bad eating habits are becoming more and more accessible by the day. Those Oreos you're craving? They're only a few steps away in the top shelf of your pantry. Those delicious salty chips you like? Yeah, they're right down the hall in a vending machine.

Heck, these days you can have your favorite fast-food delivered to your front door! All you have to do on your end is download a food delivery app, push a few buttons, then pay and someone else will do the rest. What kind of habits do you think *that* is creating in your life?

Once these eating habits start, they are *really* hard to stop; that's not just because of our lack of self-control, either. While *we* might want to alter our diet, our *body* might not. Once it becomes accustomed to something, our bodies fight back when changes happen. If you go from eating hearty burgers and fries every night to eating a salad, you can bet your body will react. Your body is a well-oiled machine of repetition. Once you give it a recurring path to walk down, it begins to do it without you even thinking about it.

I like the way that Stephen Graef, a sports psychologist at the Ohio State University Wexner Medical Center, phrased it: "Humans like to exist on autopilot." Our bodies are no different.[4]

I firmly believe that before we can alter our nutrition from one extreme to the next, we first have to understand what makes us *tick*. Where are these bad habits coming from?

Most of you have heard of Ivan Pavlov, the Russian physiologist, and his infamous Classical Conditioning Theory that was tested on his dogs. What most people don't realize is that the results of this test were a *mistake*.

Originally, Pavlov predicted that the dogs would start salivating once they saw food placed in front of them. What he actually found was that his pups were salivating as soon as they heard his assistant's footsteps, who was tasked with bringing them the food. Clever dogs![5]

Our eating habits aren't much different. You'd be surprised at how insignificant the cue could be that triggers your eating habits. You should study yourself to find out your cues. Write down every time that you go to reach for a snack in the next few days.

I'll use myself as an example. I used to have this *really* bad habit of reaching into the pantry for a small (but calorically-dense) snack every evening. Even when I was trying to cut back on calories, it never failed. Around 7:30 p.m. or 8 p.m. each night, there I was, reaching for the pantry.

I tried *everything*. I'd push back my dinner to later in the evening in order to curb my appetite, but no luck. I'd have a protein shake around 7 p.m. to try and end the night on a strong note—again, nothing.

Finally, I realized what my problem was; I wasn't reaching for the cookies, chips or desserts because I was hungry—I was grabbing a snack simply because I was bored. That's it!

I finally figured it out when I noticed that I'd grab a snack, then start scrolling through my phone—which is another sign that I'm bored.

Do you know what I did to *finally* end that terrible habit? I made sure I was doing something constructive around that time each night; I'd do some chores, I'd read a book or I'd play with my son. Almost instantly, I stopped snacking at night. How *crazy* is that?

Unfortunately, not all of my eating habits can be solved by playing with my son, Ash; I wish it were that simple! It's up to us to figure out what the root of the problem *really* is with each eating habit, then take action to fix it. If we're going to have successful self-discipline, we have to get our food consumption under control; it drives everything else that we do.

IV. The Power of Scheduling Your Meals

As I've mentioned before—and I can't stress this enough—I'm not a dietician. This Nutrition Chapter is focused on how nutrition correlates to self-discipline; it's not a recommendation on how you should eat or the ways that you'll see major improvements.

With that said, this is the only part of the chapter where I'll share some ideas on how to take back control of your nutrition. My goal here is to help *you* control your appetite, not the other way around.

Just like we learned in the Preparation Phase, the key to conquering any goal is to establish a vision, set your goals, organize those goals and your daily schedule then remove any distractions or hindrances from allowing you to achieve them.

I've spent my entire adult life focusing on how to control my diet. Five years ago, I figured out the key to doing that: organizing my eating windows. In other words, I limit myself to a few times each day where I can eat. These eating windows don't necessarily have a strict time; however, as I mentioned before, I intermittent fast, so my eating window each day is between noon and 8 p.m.

Within that eight-hour period, I generally like to limit myself to three different eating windows; I've found that this helps me eliminate needless snacking—one of the most detrimental diet-killers in most people's lives.

But my "nutrition organization"—if you want to call it that—doesn't stop there. I also keep a close eye on the calories I'm taking in each day. I've calculated my Total Daily Energy Expenditure to ensure I'm consuming the right amount of calories each day, leading to my fitness goals.

To some of you, that regimen might seem over-the-top; only a few years ago, I would have agreed with you.

But if you're willing to implement eating windows into your life, I promise you two things:

1. You'll start seeing the results you want
2. In time, this regimen will become like second nature to you

So how can you start to schedule your meals each day? I have a few steps you can take to get started.

Step One: Write Out Your Daily Schedule

First, let's start by taking out a notepad (the Notes app on your phone works, too), and jotting down your typical day, hour by hour. Here are a few questions you can ask while building your average daily schedule:

- When do you usually wake up?
- When do you typically begin your work day?
- Do you eat breakfast every morning? If so, when?
- Does your weekend routine differ much from your routine during the work week?
- What time do you usually take a lunch break?
- What time do you usually get home each night?
- When is your busiest time each day?
- Does your current meal plan instruct you to fast or stop eating at any point?
- What time of day/night do you usually find yourself reaching for a snack?

Step Two: Establish Your Ideal Number of Eating Windows

Once you have your daily agenda written down and in front of you, take the time to consider how many different eating windows you'll allow yourself each day. Ask yourself these questions:

- How many times will I allow myself to consume calories each day?
- How many eating windows would work with my typical schedule each day?
- How do I need to spread these eating windows out in order to avoid snacking?

Step Three: Find Your Total Daily Energy Expenditure

Now you have the number of eating windows you're going to allow yourself from this day forward. By this point, you'll start to see how your eating windows will help you reprioritize your life around productivity and fulfillment, rather than reaching for food every time you're bored.

Now it's time to calculate your Total Daily Energy Expenditure; this is the number of calories that your body burns in a single day. Don't worry, this won't require any mathematical prowess on your end. There are several

TDEE calculators that you can find and use online for free. Trust me, I've used them for years! Visit tdeecalculator.net for a free version you can use.

By answering a few simple questions—your gender, age, weight, height and activity level—the TDEE calculator will be able to show you your Total Daily Energy Expenditure.

The TDEE calculator will give you your maintenance calories—the number of calories that you can consume in any given day and still maintain your current weight. I realize this isn't the goal for some of you, so bear with me.

Knowing your maintenance calorie amount, you can now adjust your caloric intake to either lose weight, bulk up or—as we mentioned—maintain your current weight.

If you're looking to lose weight, experts recommend you try to consume 500 fewer calories each day than your maintenance level; this will allow you to lose up to one pound per week, while still consuming a safe amount of calories every day.

If you're interested in bulking up, then do the opposite; aim to consume 500 *more* calories each day than your maintenance level.

Step Four: Divide Your Calories Among Your Eating Windows

After you have the exact caloric intake you need to shoot for each day, all that's left to do is plug them into your daily eating windows.

I personally recommend starting by evenly dividing the amount of calories among your different eating windows to start. The math for this is simple; just take the number of your total daily calories, then divide it by the number of eating windows you're allowing yourself from now on.

You can always adjust them as need be. For example, perhaps you're not an overly big fan of breakfast. If not, then you can lower the amount you consume each morning, then add it to your lunch, dinner, etc. Here are a few questions you can ask yourself when dividing up your calories:

- Is there a time of day when I don't typically consume many calories?
- Do I typically eat more during the morning, mid-day, or evening?
- How can I divvy up my calories to prevent myself from snacking?
- How many calories are optimal for each eating window depending on my schedule?

Whether you like it or not, your nutrition and self-discipline are forever intertwined. Those that learn this and take control of it are the ones that breed a healthy and successful lifestyle.

Granted, a poor diet doesn't mean you'll be unsuccessful. Warren Buffett, one of the most successful businessmen of all time has mentioned his unusual—and vastly unhealthy—diet. He eats mostly McDonald's, drinks several Coca-Cola beverages and gets ice cream almost every day. More power to him, but that's not how I choose to live my life.

I want to feel *good* each day. I want balance in my nutrition. In order to reach my goals, I *need* consistent energy levels from the food I eat. If limiting the foods I eat and scheduling my meals each day is the price to pay, then I'll take that every day of the week.

But let me stress this to you: it's important to *reward yourself*. You shouldn't feel ashamed if you start trying to eat a healthy diet, then have a few too many slices of pizza one night or eat an entire pint of ice cream in one sitting. If there is anything I've learned about nutrition, it's that nobody bats a thousand.

I'm not saying you have to, but I typically allow myself one cheat meal each week. I typically take it each Saturday, so that I can reward myself for working hard and abiding by my meal plan during the work week.

But I'll tell you this, I don't let my diet consume me. If my wife and I go meet friends at a restaurant on a Wednesday night, I'm not going to restrict myself to the salad menu. I try to be conscious of what I eat and not overexert myself. Even if I do "cheat," I wake up the next day and set out to right the ship again.

On your nutrition journey, you'll come across many hurdles. Don't let that deter you. Correct your eating windows when they need to be corrected and clean up your diet when it needs to be cleaned up; that's the lesson here. When we're climbing our Self-Discipline Tree, we need to continuously adapt to overcome branches that seem out of reach.

CHAPTER 7

WELL-BEING

If you're a Millennial (anyone born between 1981 and 1996), or the parent of one, then you've undoubtedly seen the kids TV series *Arthur*. It follows the daily adventures of Arthur the aardvark, his family and all of his friends.

Growing up, Arthur taught me many of life's greatest lessons (I'm only half kidding). But, perhaps, his greatest lesson came before the episode technically started—from the show's theme song.

I'm going to break down some of the lyrics—if you know the song, feel free to sing along!

> *And I say HEY! (HEY!)*
> *What a wonderful kind of day.*
> *If you can learn to work and play,*
> *And get along with each other.*

That chorus, to me, perfectly sums up how we can ensure a happy, healthy life for ourselves: it's all up to us. *We* control how we perceive our lives. If we can "learn to work and play" like the chorus states, then you'll experience a "wonderful kind of day."

Be honest with yourself, have you learned to work and play? Or do you find yourself getting into your car every work day dreading the nine-to-five job that you're showing up to? *It shouldn't be that way.*

If you don't find value in your job or have the ability to enjoy what you do, you'll never achieve self-discipline. Why? Because you'll never be *inspired* to.

It's like the old adage goes, "If you find a career that you love, you'll never work a day in your life." I'm happiest and most productive when I'm doing something I love, like writing this book! I hope you can find that for yourself as well.

The theme song also has another nugget of advice hidden in the song's bridge that pertains to successful self-discipline:

> *It's a simple message and it comes from the heart,*
> *Believe in yourself (believe in yourself),*
> *Well, that's the place to start (to start).*[1]

Arthur is *preaching*, isn't he? It's a simple message. It's a simple concept: just believe in yourself—that's where it all starts!

If you're going to develop successful self-discipline and climb your tree, then you have to start by believing in yourself. I love the quote from legendary boxer Sugar Ray Robinson, "To be a champ, you have to believe in yourself when no one else will." If anyone knows about being a champ, it was this International Boxing Hall of Famer.[2]

I'm a firm believer that you *cannot* maintain self-discipline without prioritizing your own well-being; the two go hand-in-hand. If you aren't taking care of yourself and your mindset, then you won't have inspiration to stick to a structured routine. As we talked about in the very first chapter, inspiration is a key element to successful self-discipline.

But how can we get to a state of well-being? There are a few moving pieces, but it all starts with adopting the right mindset. Let's start there!

I. Finding the Optimal Mindset

This might not be comforting to you, but the more you work towards accomplishing your goals, the more likely you'll be to hit a bump in the road. Does that scare you? It shouldn't.

Everyone that drives down the road of life gets a flat tire now and again. But are you just going to pull off to the side of the road and quit? If you're taking the time to read this book, I'd venture to guess you're the type of person that won't get deflated.

Here's my mindset when I pop a tire in my metaphorical "life car"— I'll just switch out the tire and keep going, and if I run out of spare tires, then I'll just walk the rest of the way. I won't quit, and neither will you!

But where does all this drive—pun intended—come from? What are the key elements to a healthy mindset? How can we keep the proper viewpoint when the going gets tough? There are a few contributing factors.

Think about this, the person that you'll be five years from now is dependent on the choices you make right now. Do you want to be happy and healthy in five years? Great! It all starts with *today*.

Let's look at the different elements we have to establish in our lives in order to achieve a happy, healthy and hungry mindset.

Mindset Element #1: Optimism

Imagine you've set out to climb to the top of a mountain. You slowly but surely make your way up, stopping for a few breaks along the way. Depending on the size of the mountain, you might even set up camp for a night or two. Finally, after a lot of hard work and dedication, you make it to the top. Once you're at the top of the mountain, are you the type to say, "Wow, this is a beautiful view" or "Ugh… that's a long way back down to the bottom"? Be honest. Your answer says a lot about your current mindset.

Some of you might say that your response to the mountain question depends on the day, and that's fair! We all experience good and bad days.

But I want to challenge you here… Do you think it's impossible to keep an optimistic viewpoint while you're having a bad day? If you said "yes," you're wrong.

Too often, people get the definition of "optimism" wrong; they think it means that you're *always happy*. News flash: it doesn't. Having optimism simply means that you're hopeful and confident about the future.

Even on my worst days, I'm optimistic; that doesn't mean I've got a smile on my face when my car full of groceries won't start in the middle of a Costco parking lot—it just means that I know this moment will pass.

This doesn't come easily for some people. If you find yourself a part of that camp, then I have an exercise you can try.

Any time you catch yourself starting a sentence with "I have to," replace it with "I *get* to." Doing this ensures that no matter what you say after those three words, there's an optimistic spin to it.

Let's try it! I *get* to go to work today because I'm lucky to have a job while many people don't; I *get* to mow the lawn because I'm fortunate enough to have a lawn to mow and the tools to mow it. Dare I write this next one down (when I know my wife will read it)? I *get* to change my son's diaper because I'm lucky to have a happy, healthy baby who is in great health and poops—a lot, I might add.

You see what I mean? Even the most daunting of tasks can have an appreciative side to them if we give ourselves the chance to look at them that way.

There's another aspect to optimism that I want to tackle before we move on, and that's getting rid of the *"grass is greener on the other side"* mentality.

We've all heard that expression before, and yet we're all guilty of feeling that way. Every single day we envy other people, other jobs, other spouses (uh-oh!), other people's possessions… the list goes on and on.

Can I share a nugget of knowledge with you? That mindset is *poisoning* your self-discipline; it's a sign that you don't have optimism in your life. Let's start correcting that right now. Pull out the Notes app on your phone and make a list of five things that you're grateful for at this very moment.

Feel better?

Maintaining an optimistic perspective isn't easy when other people in our lives seem to be thriving more than we are—I get it—but the very fact that you're coveting someone else's life is proof that you aren't optimistic about your own.

Everyone has things that they want to accomplish, but haven't yet. And that's a *good* thing! It means that you have things to work towards and that you won't remain stagnant because you'll be striving to improve yourself and your life.

Just because your best friend is happily married with two beautiful kids doesn't mean that *you* should be married with kids at this point in your life; everyone's path is different. I promise you, God has a plan for you, and your happy marriage is on the way!

Instead of playing the comparison game—something we all do—think about ways you can improve, and prepare for that reward for when it shows up in *your* life.

For example, if you aren't married yet, think about the type of man/woman *you* want to be when you *do* meet your soulmate. If you haven't landed that manager position yet, start conducting yourself like a boss, learn all you can and start building healthy leadership traits.

Lastly, if you're struggling to keep an optimistic mindset, I have one piece of advice for you: focus on what you *do* have. Whenever I catch myself jealous of others or impatient with my growth, I pray. I thank God for everything that I do have, and I mean *everything*. In only a minute or two, I feel relieved.

Mindset Element #2: Integrity

Growing up, my dad used to tell me: "Son, if a task is worth doing, then it's worth doing right."

In other words, if you're going to exert energy and effort into any task or job, then you shouldn't be cutting corners to accomplish it.

Think of a goal you made in our Goal-Setting Chapter. Any goal. Are you going to hold yourself accountable to seeing that goal through? Do you truly understand what it will take to achieve it? How will you stop yourself when you try to take a shortcut?

I don't know about you, but I want to be remembered as a man of integrity with any job that I do. I don't want to feel success knowing that I stepped on others to get there.

We'll talk more about integrity in our Reputation Chapter, but for now, know this: if you try to take shortcuts, it will come back to bite you. I'm a firm believer in karma; what goes around, always, always, *always* comes back around—and when it does, it will cause harm to your well-being.

Mindset Element #3: Respectfulness

When I was a kid, my church had a program where a few members of the church would make a bag of cookies and deliver them to all first-time visitors each week.

They struggled to find consistent volunteers to deliver those cookies, so my dad would step up when they needed an extra hand.

Generally, he would deliver the cookies after I had practice. We were already out—why not kill two birds with one stone, right?

The job was simple: pick up the cookies from church, drive to each guest's house (they willingly gave this information out on our church's welcome cards, by the way), knock on the door, say "Thank you for attending service," and then make their day by handing them a bag full of cookies.

I *hated* doing this.

Mind you, this was back before we had maps on our phones, so the only way we'd be able to find a house was by pulling out a giant map of Florissant, Missouri, and making several wrong turns until we found the correct house.

Growing up, I never understood *why* my dad would volunteer for this task time and time again. How could he possibly *enjoy* this?

Now I realize that he didn't do it because he enjoyed it; he did it because it needed to be done. The cookies were a way to show our first-time visitors that they were welcome in our church.

As a result, those first-time guests would often come back to attend another service. Why? Because we showed them respect and appreciation.

Here's another example. One of our closest family friends is the epitome of what it means to climb the ladder in a company. He started in an entry-level position in security and is now the Senior Manager of Purchasing at the same organization. How did he do it? In his own words, "By making 'respecting others' a priority."

Do you have the self-discipline in you to show others respect, even when they might not deserve it? Can you swallow your pride enough to avoid being overly competitive in your conversations with others?

If not, then these things will quickly tarnish your own reputation. Treating others with respect is one of the few chances we get to show our self-discipline to other people.

Respectfulness generates reward. Though it may not feel like others notice the effort you're making to show respect to difficult people, they do, and your stock will skyrocket because of it.

Mindset Element #4: Trust

Trusting others is difficult enough. But trusting yourself? That can be even harder. If you're going to enter a new echelon of well-being, then self-trust *has* to be prioritized.

I'll keep this short and sweet: without trust, you won't be able to accomplish what you want to in life.

When referring to successful self-discipline, I'm a big believer that there are three forms of trust we need: trust in ourselves, trust in the goals you've set and trust in those around you.

Maybe you've been burned in the past by trusting others—let it go. Perhaps you've failed at so many projects that you feel like you can't trust yourself—put it behind you. If you're going to achieve your goals, it will be because you had the ability to *trust*.

Mindset Element #5: Self-Esteem

Here's another reason why trusting yourself is important: without it, you'll never be able to build self-esteem.

Most of us know that self-esteem is essentially the confidence we have in ourselves—however—it goes beyond that. Self-esteem is having the confidence in your skills—it's knowing that you bring something to the table that no one else can.

Once you realize you have unique skills, you start to build respect for yourself (self-respect). That respect turns into confidence, and that confidence turns into growth.

In my eyes, self-esteem is all about being good to yourself. As you pursue your goals, there will be days where you fail. Will you let those change your perception of yourself? There will be days when you feel uninspired and want to sleep in. Should that derail how you perceive yourself? Of course not.

Successful self-discipline is all about maintaining a positive attitude. If you let negativity creep in, the first thing it will go after is your self-esteem—I promise you that!

When it comes to self-esteem, just remember this: you're a shepherd, not a lion tamer. In other words, there will be times when you'll wander off the path and get lost; you're going to have to guide yourself, and your thoughts, back to the path just like a shepherd would.

Mindset Element #6: Willpower

In order to use willpower to your advantage, you have to first understand it. Many people look at willpower as a skill that few people possess; that definition is wrong in two ways. First, it isn't a skill. Second, we all possess it *and* can harness it if we understand how it works.

In his book *The Power of Habit*, Charles Duhigg explains an experiment that researchers once performed on college students to test the application of willpower.

The experiment was simple: for each student, they'd sit them at a table with two plates in front of them. One plate had radishes, the other had cookies.

To learn more about willpower, the researchers would instruct half of the students to only eat the cookies, and the other half of the students to only eat the radishes (poor kids!).

After five minutes, the researchers would come back into the room and require each student to solve a puzzle (which the students didn't realize was actually unsolvable). "If you want to quit," the researchers told the students, "all you have to do is ring the bell."

On average, the cookie-eaters spent *twice* as long working to solve the unsolvable puzzle than the radish-eaters.

Why? Because the radish-eaters had mentally drained themselves by having to refrain from eating the delicious plate of cookies in front of them. By the time the puzzle was handed to them, they had run out of willpower.

The cookie-eaters, on the other hand, had more willpower to use towards the puzzle since they didn't have to use it refusing the cookies. The study showed that it's easy to refrain from eating radishes—I'm kidding!

What the study actually showed was this: willpower isn't a skill, it's a muscle. Just like any other muscle that undergoes an immense amount of work, it tires out and has little energy to use towards other things.

Mark Muraven, the leading researcher on this experiment, gave some insight into using willpower towards your goals or tasks. He said, "If you want to do something that requires willpower—like going for a run after work—you have to conserve your willpower muscle during the day."

He went on to tell Duhigg, "If you use it up too early on tedious tasks like writing emails or filling out expense forms, all the strength will be gone by the time you get home."[3]

Mindset Element #7: Focus

If the story of my life can offer any lessons, it's this: focus is a key factor in success. When I was without focus in my high school years, I failed at nearly everything that I touched. I gained the ability to focus (when I finally decided to apply myself) during my freshman year of community college—thank God—and haven't looked back since.

There's another word I use for how focus applies to the goals we're trying to accomplish—concentration.

Can you concentrate on long-term goals that you are years out from getting accomplished? Do you have the ability to focus on short-term goals and work towards them every day, thus turning your long-term goals into a reality?

Here's the reassuring part: we don't have to be focused 24 hours a day to get the results that we want; that would be impossible for everyone—I don't care *who* you are.

All you need is to prioritize a little bit of deep focus (aka "deep work") each day. If you can do that, I guarantee you you'll accomplish any goal that you set.

So how much deep focus should we shoot for? Contrary to popular belief, eight hours isn't our goal here. Modern research has shown that you only need three to four hours of deep work each day to make significant progress.[4]

I can almost hear a collective sigh of relief from my readers as I typed that last sentence. It gets better! That isn't on a per-goal scale.

In other words, if you have a goal of getting a promotion and a goal of losing 25 pounds, you don't need to spend three to four hours on each in order to make progress.

Divide up the amount of goals you're shooting for right now (I recommend no more than three or four at a time), then divide that number of goals by four hours; that's how much deep focus time you need to spend towards your goals (either long-term goals or short-term goals) each day. Make time for *deep* work!

II. The Power of Meditation

I'm a huge Spongebob Squarepants fan, so naturally I was going to find a way to reference the cartoon in this book. I apologize in advance if you've never seen the show before (where have you *been?*) and this reference seems like gibberish to you.

In one of the episodes, Squidward Tentacles (Spongebob's coworker) is trying to turn the Krusty Krab (the restaurant Spongebob works at) into a five-star restaurant in order to impress one of his old high school rivals, Squilliam Fancyson. To do that, he needs Spongebob to quickly become a five-star waiter and serve Squilliam's every need.

To get some perspective and prepare Spongebob for a task he's never done before, Squidward tells him to "empty his mind."

This flashes to a sequence in Spongebob's brain where millions of little Spongebobs in an office setting are running around shredding all of Spongebob's other thoughts and memories like "Jelly Fishing 101," "childhood memories," and so on, in order to help him clear his mind and focus on being the best waiter he can be.

While meditation didn't work out so well for Spongebob in the end—because he accidentally forgot everything (including his name)—it can work *wonders* for us as humans.

Imagine being able to go into your brain and shred things like "that guy that cut you off on the highway today" or "the *one* customer that cursed you out during a cold call." How much more effective would you be each day if you could eliminate those useless thoughts from your mind?

I have good news for you: you *do* have that ability. We all do. All you have to do is carve out some time each day to gather your thoughts.

When I studied all of the surveys I received from successful people in my network, I was *shocked* to see how few people prioritized finding time to meditate each day.

Part of that, I figure, is because they didn't understand my intent. When I asked how often they found time to meditate, I wonder if some of them were envisioning me sitting on a yoga mat with my eyes closed, fingers pinched together and repeating "aum" over and over again. That's not what I meant at all.

In fact, the word *meditate* is often misunderstood. People think it means finding time to relax; others think it means concentrating on your deep breathing. Those are merely a *form* of meditation.

Meditate actually means "to focus one's thoughts." In another definition, it means to "plan or project in one's mind." Tell me you couldn't use more of that in your daily life—I know I can!

Meditation is *crucial* to successful self-discipline. Without taking time to focus on your own thoughts and plan ahead, you won't have the discipline to keep pushing. Eventually, you'll lose your way.

Start by finding a way to mix your preferred form of relaxation with a constructive habit. The one recommendation I always give people is to find ways of prioritizing your Vitamin D with the form of meditation you choose.

For example, if you find that listening to certain podcasts relaxes you, then listen to a podcast while running. Not only will this help you escape for a few minutes, it will also help you look forward to that time of exercise and release more dopamine (the feel-good hormone) in your brain.

For those of you that don't know, we as humans get the most Vitamin D from exposing our skin to the sun, albeit for healthy amounts of time. What I'm proposing here is that if you have a form of meditation that you can do outside, then do so!

If you enjoy reading your Bible to find time to reflect, take it outside. If you find yoga helps you to take a few minutes to think, do some yoga on your balcony or deck.

To get enough Vitamin D each day, try to expose as much skin as possible to the sun for 10 to 30 minutes a day. Experts recommend that you try to get sun exposure around mid-day when the sun is at its peak.[5]

I'm a huge proponent that we shouldn't give ourselves only one 1-hour window each day to meditate and reflect. I think we can find more time for meditation if we break it up into smaller increments.

For example, if I told you that meditation *had* to include one hour of undisturbed quiet time, you'd never find the time for it; *maybe* during your lunch break, but probably not even then.

But if I told you that meditation can be performed in smaller windows, then you can find time for it during your ride to and from work, during part of your lunch, in 10 minute increments each hour of your work day and so on. All of a sudden, that's *way* more than one hour of collective meditation, make sense?

If you're going to find more time for meditation and reflection each day, then you *have* to prioritize it. I like to do this by looking at my day as one big calendar, then breaking it down and allocating time.

Let's start with this exercise: quickly take out a piece of paper and write down the routine that you have each day into 30-minute segments. Just so you know what I mean, you would break it up in terms of 7 a.m., 7:30 a.m., 8 a.m., 8:30 a.m. and so on.

Once you've written those segments down, describe what you do in each block of time. Here's an example from 7 a.m. to 10 a.m. back when I was a salesman:

7 a.m.: Drive to work
7:30 a.m.: (Still driving to work)
8 a.m.: Make five business to business phone calls (I'd find five businesses to call the night before)
8:30 a.m.: Answer emails
9 a.m.: Make 10 cold calls
9:30 a.m.: Prospect and answer emails
10 a.m.: Make 10 cold calls

After you've broken up your day and described what you do in each 30-minute window, try to identify some times that you could meditate—even for five minutes—and describe what you could do to gather your thoughts. This could include things like saying a quick prayer, stretching, listening to a meditation app, doing some deep breathing and so on. Whatever you'd like to do and have the time for, do it, but try to mix it up!

By organizing your day and intentionally writing down when you expect to meditate and reflect, you'll be much more likely to find the time.

The one thing I prioritize each day is what I call the "First 5." I'm referring to the first five minutes after I wake up, but the title just makes it *sound* cooler!

What I do with that first five minutes, in my mind, dictates how the rest of my day will go.

As you might imagine, my work day can get pretty hectic between writing seven articles each day for my career, raising a child and working on my business.

I like to take those first five minutes to open up the Bible app on my phone and read part of a daily devotion. Naturally, that devotion includes a devotional piece and at least one to two bible verses. After I've read the devotional, I pray to thank God for all he's given me, and to ask that he help me maintain focus throughout my day.

The First 5, in my mind, is a perfect window of time; it's short enough that I can stick to it every day, but long enough for me to get what I need before I hop up out of bed.

III. Faith

One Sunday morning, the lead pastor at my church was preaching about the modern day spirit. He stepped on stage as he normally would, but with a table set up behind him.

He uncovered the table to reveal a record player, a tape recorder, a CD player, an iPod and an Alexa device, all sitting side by side—in that order.

He began by going up to the record player and playing *Ain't No Mountain High Enough* by The Temptations. Then, with the record player still blasting tunes, he went over to the tape player and turned on *I'll Be There For You* by Bon Jovi.

Keeping those two songs blaring, he then walked over to the CD player and turned on *Oops!... I Did It Again* by Britney Spears.

With Britney added to the mix, he then turned to the iPod and played *I Gotta Feeling* by the Black Eyed Peas.

Finally, he leaned over to the Alexa device and requested that it play *The Blessing* by Elevation Worship.

With all of those songs *still* playing, he stood on stage and let the songs blare for a few seconds. He must've looked out to the crowd and seen a sea of people giving him strange looks—I know *I* was!

After about five seconds, he turned to the crowd and said, "*This* is what our souls sound like today."

He was insinuating that if we could hear what our souls sounded like, it would sound like a jumbled mess. Why? Because we push and pull it in so many different directions throughout the day.

We set physical goals for ourselves, we establish long-term and short-term goals to advance in our career, but few of us ever take the time to establish *faith*-based goals for ourselves. We never think twice about how we can improve the health of our souls, the only thing we get to keep after this life is over!

As the old saying goes, "If you aren't improving, then you're regressing." There is no "staying the same," it doesn't work like that.

In the same sermon, our head pastor challenged us with this question: "If your physical nature reflected the nourishment of your spiritual nature, would we immediately send you to the hospital?" You're the only one who knows the answer.

The connection between faith and successful self-discipline is undeniable. Faith gives you vision and a respect for others that you wouldn't otherwise have. This world doesn't teach us how to view things from an eternal perspective; it teaches us to focus solely on the materials and money that we "should" collect in this life, and we fall for it too often.

Faith builds the foundation for self-discipline. Once you have that viewpoint that few others have in this life, your mannerisms and poise will become noticeable to others. Self-respect and self-accountability become that much more natural, I've found, when you have your eyes fixed on setting a strong example for others.

For me, it all starts with prayer. Prayer grounds me in a way that nothing else can. Those of us that have the privilege of doing it know how much a simple prayer can resonate with us.

Prayer grants you with perspective and helps you take back control of your life. I can't tell you how many times I've prayed for something and, in hearing myself say it out loud, realized how petty or foolish it was. Prayer refreshes and resets me.

It also helps free you of stress. For those of you that have never *tried* praying before, or haven't done it in a while, I urge you to give it another shot. You won't feel stressed about the things outside of your control. You'll have much more peace of mind when you leave those external factors up to God.

Lastly, prayer helps grant you confidence. There's beauty in the action of letting go. How great does this sound? God will take care of the things that you *can't* control; all you have to do is work hard on the things that you *can* control. Sounds pretty freeing, right?

I don't know if you're religious or not, but know this: whether you are or aren't religious, I've been praying for you every single night while writing this book. I hope you find comfort in that!

The last thing I want to mention here is the power I've found in reading the Bible; it helps you follow what God has called you to do. You'd be shocked at how many times I've opened the Bible and started reading a chapter or verse that applied to the *exact thing* I was struggling with.

The very book that you're reading is a product from God. This book on self-discipline has come from hours of prayer and reading the Bible. I don't know about you, but I wouldn't want to read a self-empowering book that stemmed from anywhere else!

IV. Balancing Self-Discipline and Enjoying Life

If we're being honest, most of us think of the word "discipline" with a negative connotation tied to it; we think back to our days of getting grounded for not unloading the dishwasher. Then, you add the word "self" in front of it, and suddenly we think the word "self-discipline" means punishing ourselves.

I'm here to tell you that it's quite the opposite. Having more self-discipline makes life more fulfilling and joyful.

Think of it this way: day in and day out, you hold yourself accountable to working towards your goals. Then, one day, you look up and see how far you've come. Meanwhile, all your other friends and colleagues were stagnant and complacent. Tell me that wouldn't feel good!

Successful self-discipline doesn't require you to be your own drill sergeant. By having more self-discipline, you'll find more time to enjoy the things you love and you'll be better equipped to prioritize work-life balance. I'd argue that *that* is the most important part of this whole journey.

We all focus on having enough self-discipline to continually work towards bettering our careers, but there's *two* sides to that coin; you also have to have the self-discipline to force yourself to clock out.

Whenever you clock out for the night, completely disconnect yourself. If you don't, then work will consume you and you'll struggle to find self-discipline in areas other than your profession. Ask any of the millions of businessmen/businesswomen that get divorced or become detached from their children because they obsess over work.

So here's my solution for you; in order to prioritize time to disconnect and keep perspective, you should allow yourself what I like to call an "Emergency Break Period," or EBP for short.

An EBP is a time period of five minutes in which you allow yourself to walk away from everything. These are similar to the meditation breaks that we mentioned in the Power of Meditation header in this chapter, except EBPs aren't predetermined; they're used as a last-minute solution if you find yourself frustrated, overwhelmed or bored.

If you wish to take an Emergency Break Period, then there's only one condition: you have to stimulate all five senses before you get back to what you were doing. If you need a reminder, the five senses are sight, sound, smell, taste, and touch. Here's an example of what I mean:

SIGHT - Look at a picture that makes you smile.
SOUND - Listen to a song that conjures up some positive nostalgia.
SMELL - Light a candle or go outside and smell the fresh air, etc.

TASTE - Chew a piece of gum or make a protein shake (my personal favorite).

TOUCH - Pet your dog or rub a soft blanket (it helps, trust me!)

I know, I know. Some of you might be thinking this sounds crazy, but I promise that it works.

The next time you feel overly frustrated over a petty customer complaint or after interacting with a manager you don't respect, disconnect yourself for five minutes and perform an Emergency Break Period. I guarantee you'll come back to your desk with a fresh perspective and a calm demeanor.

What I want for us all, more than anything, is to maintain a sense of well-being as we improve our self-discipline. If we don't, then what's the point of any of this?

If you can empower yourself to climb your Self-Discipline Tree and take active steps towards your goals with a sound mind, there is *nothing* you can't accomplish; no long-term goal will seem out of reach; no short-term goal will feel like a waste of time. You'll be intentional, focused and most importantly, happy.

In my short but successful career thus far, I've lived in five different cities throughout the country. I've met people with different job titles, backgrounds, ethnicities and pathways to success. The only people that are *truly* happy are those who are unwilling to sacrifice their work-life balance.

I've seen Chief-level personnel intentionally decline a meeting because they "got to" coach their child's soccer team. I've talked to entrepreneurs who purposely don't interact with social media on the weekends. Why? Because they knew that their business goals and ambitions would still be there in the morning or the following Monday when they returned to work. They'd tackle them then, and with more focus and energy than if they'd stretched their willpower too thin—as we discussed earlier in this chapter.

Always focus on the well-being of yourself and those you care about most. Everything else—your career, your goals, your future successes—are nothing without having a positive perspective and a sense of well-being.

Chapter 8

EXECUTION

Up until now, you and I have learned how to envision success, set the goals we want to achieve, organize those goals, get rid of potential setbacks and distractions and work towards our goals in a way that's both inspiring and fulfilling.

Now that we have all of this information under our belts, there's only one thing left to do: carry out the plan.

You hear it all the time in sports; watch any post-game press conference of a coach or player on the losing team and they all say some variation of the same thing, "We didn't execute the game plan."

Perhaps before reading this book, you had no idea how to properly establish your goals or proactively avoid potential setbacks. Well, now you do. But what do you intend to *do* with that?

Do you really want to look back years from now and tell yourself that, even though you *knew* how to accomplish your long-term goals, you simply didn't because you didn't execute your game plan? I think I know your answer.

I say this as a guy that's been there—it's the *lowest* feeling in the world; worse than losing to a buzzer-beater shot from the other team; worse than getting dumped by an old girlfriend or boyfriend; worse than having someone look you square in the eye and say, "You'll never amount to anything."

Why? Because those are factors you *can't* control. Whether you end up executing the plan you've created or not is solely up to you. It isn't because you're incapable of executing the plan, it's because you lacked the self-discipline to see it through.

Fortunately for you and I, successful self-discipline can be taught! It doesn't happen overnight, but if you *really* work at it, then that self-discipline will start to become natural.

Even better news: we can teach ourselves how to prioritize and establish successful self-discipline as we climb towards our goals. Let's start by jumping into some concrete methods for building structure into our lives.

I. Teaching Yourself Self-Discipline

Here's the thing about self-discipline—most of us already have a pretty good understanding of what it looks like. If you offer a friend a cookie and they say "No thanks, I'm trying to lose weight," *that's* self-discipline.

So why do so many of us not use it? I've come to find that it's because a vast majority of us don't understand the different components.

Going back to our health-conscious friend who refused the cookie for a moment, there are many different layers that led to him getting to that level of self-discipline.

Even with just those seven words, our friend accomplished several things ahead of staying resolute to his goals: he established momentum for himself, made a conscious decision to set excuses aside and established firm resiliency for his goal of losing weight and keeping it off. Let's go over those three factors in a bit more detail to learn how we can slowly start to teach ourselves self-discipline.

Factor #1: Establish Momentum for Yourself

As I just mentioned, self-discipline doesn't happen instantaneously; nothing that's worth our time does—it takes time and effort. But do you know what those two things create when they're done together? Momentum!

Momentum is a disciplined person's best friend. It confirms that they're on their way towards achieving their goals.

These little checkpoints are what most people refer to as "small wins." Most of you probably think that's a stupid expression created by your managers to build team chemistry, but trust me, it's a real thing.

Let's use losing weight as an example as it's a prime goal for most people. In order to lose weight, you have to intentionally keep yourself at a caloric deficit each day; that's quite an adjustment for those of us who are fortunate to have food available to us whenever we want.

Being in a caloric deficit at the end of the day is tough for the first few days. However, once you start to see your face slim up or the number on the scale get lower and lower, you gain more confidence and excitement for what's ahead. That declining number on the scale is confirmation that you're on your way to achieving your goals.

Remember that Bing-Goal Board we made in Chapter 3? This is one of the main reasons it's so useful. As you begin to cross more and more small goals off of your Bing-Goal Board, you'll gain more confidence and momentum, thus naturally generating more self-discipline. Why? Because, in our heads, that self-discipline is now justified through results we've witnessed.

Factor #2: Set the Excuses Aside

It doesn't matter who you are or how successful you've been up to this point, there will always be the temptation to make excuses. If I were to gather a list of all the goals

I've failed to achieve in my life, I'd venture to guess that 99-percent of them were because I made excuses to not try; in other words, my failure was self-inflicted.

Excuses are the bane of our personal lives. We get home from our nine-to-five and make every excuse in the book not to chase our dreams—whether that be the dream to build your own business, get back into shape, or anything else.

Here's my plea to you: work on implementing self-discipline into every area of your life, not just the part of your life that you have a position/title for. It's easier to have discipline in a job where you're held accountable for your performance. But when you can establish self-discipline behind closed doors—that's when the magic happens!

Self-discipline starts when we tell ourselves that we're setting aside all of our usual excuses. Here's another term for excuses: *lies.* We *lie* to ourselves when we say we have no more "gas left in the tank" to go for a run after work. Save some willpower in your day for the run you plan to take later that night—as we discussed in the last chapter.

We *lie* to ourselves when we say we'll never be able to achieve something; only small minds truly think that. *You* reading this book is proof that you don't truly believe you're incapable of accomplishing your goals and dreams. Put those excuses—lies—to bed. We have work to do!

Factor #3: Establish Resiliency in Your Life

On January 3rd, 2019, the St. Louis Blues were ranked dead last in the entire National Hockey League. With just a little over half of the season remaining, the Blues had to make a choice: quit on that season and trade away some of their star players, or stick it out. They chose the latter.

Only five months later, they won the Stanley Cup for the first time in the franchise's 49-year history. How were they able to pull off such a tremendous feat? Their players and coaches said it best: "with resilience."[1]

From the outside looking in, that turnaround seems like quite the accomplishment. However, everyone inside the locker room knew the same thing: they were capable of winning the entire time. They had the talent to go on a winning streak *months* before, all they needed was to establish a foundation that they could build on.

That's the truth for all of us, isn't it? We all know that we have what it takes to reach the goals we've set: installing a resolute and unwavering mindset that you will not walk away from this goal until you achieve it.

Everyone loves a good come-back story, but here's the thing—you can achieve success from the get-go if you establish resiliency. You have ability to bounce back from any difficulty that you face, dust your shoulders off and continue pushing towards your goals.

Know that you'll take a few hits along the way, though. There will be times when you have to run through what feels like a gauntlet to get to where you need to go. But if you make a conscious decision now to not back down, you've already established the self-discipline that you can build off of!

II. How to "Walk the Walk"

Raise your hand if you enjoy taking instructions from people that don't practice what they preach. We all know those people who are quick to bark out orders, but don't apply that knowledge to their own lives. They dish it out, but they can't take it.

I hate to tell you, my friend, but if you've set goals for yourself and you aren't working towards them—in some capacity—each day, then you would be considered one of those people; we're all guilty of it.

Self-discipline is all about taking *action;* it's about taking those goals that we set in Chapter 2 and organized in Chapter 3, then carrying out the plan.

It's time that we establish a "start today" mindset in our lives; no more waiting for tomorrow. **Start your goals right here and now.** Set this book down and perform one *tiny* act towards your short-term goals, if that's what it takes.

People often say, *"I'll start my weight loss after the holiday season is over."* No! Start right now! Purchase a workout routine. Go for a run. Read an article about how to correct your diet; these are small tasks you can accomplish *right now*.

Start by determining a few "non-negotiables" for the day ahead—these are tiny goals that you *refuse* to not have completed, or at least put effort into, by the time the day is through.

For example, my non-negotiables are my faith and my family. I never go a day without reading at least one Bible verse or saying at least three prayers—one in the morning, afternoon and night, then more as need be. I never go a day without telling my wife and son I love them. My weekends are dedicated to family time; no work talk allowed.

Exercise is very close to being a non-negotiable for me, but I give myself a *tiny* bit of leeway under extreme circumstances, especially since rest days are a vital part of any healthy exercise routine. With that said, I never go two consecutive days without a workout to avoid falling off the wagon.

But action without repetition gains zero momentum. In my opinion, you can't be self-disciplined if you lack consistency. As a Millennial, I always think back to the TV show *Pinky and the Brain* as the leading example of what it truly means to remain consistent.

No matter how unsuccessful those lab mice were the day before or what went wrong in their previous plot, they always had the same goal—say it with me at home—"To try and take over the world!"

Isn't that what we're all working towards, here? Not taking over the world, but to be exactly like Brain and wake up knowing *exactly* what we want to achieve? *Imagine* what you could accomplish.

Consistency is crucial to developing positive habits, leading to better execution every day; it helps you prioritize your goals even when life throws you twists and turns. As we all know, once we've taken even one or two days off, it's hard to get back in a rhythm without discipline and vision.

In order to start walking the walk with your self-discipline, start by doing the three things I just mentioned: establish a "start today" mindset, list out a few non-negotiable tasks each day and prioritize consistency. Everything else will start to fall into place.

III. Finding Your Competition

I'm as competitive as they come. Ask anyone that knows me well and they'll all tell you the same thing—I *hate* when someone beats me at something; it's never an easy pill for me to swallow. With that said, I've learned when to turn that competitive side off and on for the sake of my own well-being. Not everything in life should be a competition.

There are two forms of competition: healthy competition and unhealthy competition. I hope I don't have to tell you which one you'll need to pursue.

Unhealthy competition is when someone intentionally tries to skew the playing field in their favor to avoid losing; this could either be by cutting corners—otherwise known as *"cheating"*—or seeking out competitors that you know aren't up to your level.

Healthy competition, on the other hand, embraces the challenge; it's when you push yourself against the best in order to reach new heights. Even if you don't come out on top, you show joy and respect for the person/people that did.

No matter what you're doing, there's some form of competition going on inside your head—whether you know it or not.

If you're a salesman/saleswoman, then there's a competition amongst you and your coworkers to surpass new sales goals. If you're on a sports team, you're competing against both the opponent (to win the game) as well as your teammates (to score the most goals, have the most assists, have the best batting average and so on).

You can choose to let that competition turn into either a healthy or unhealthy thing, but it can never be both.

I was never the most talented midfielder on my college lacrosse team, not by a long shot. Guys were faster, stronger, had a better shot—you name it. I chose to turn my shortcomings into healthy competition between myself and everyone else at practice. When someone else came on top, I was legitimately happy for them; it's what got me the honor of becoming a Team Captain, even as a defensive midfielder.

One of the biggest lies in our society is that not winning the competition makes you a failure. Failure, when used constructively, leads to success.

Back when I was in ticket sales, I beat out one of my coworkers for the most revenue in our office one season. After barely coming in second, that coworker worked his tail off the next offseason and *blew* past me in revenue only a few months later. Right after passing my numbers, he got promoted to a premium sales position where he now focuses on selling club seats and luxury suites.

His self-discipline and drive propelled him to a position that usually takes *much* longer to obtain. Could anyone say that he *lost* by coming in second to me that one season? I don't think so!

If you come in second, third, or fourth from healthy competition, make a vow to yourself that it will never happen again.

IV. Serve-First Mindset

When most of us think about success, we envision a man or woman standing atop an Olympic-style pedestal with everyone else looking up at them from below. In other words, we assume that successful people are the ones that put their heads down and looked out for themselves. However, success—*true* success—comes from contributing more to other people's lives than your own.

The infamous author H. Jackson Brown, Jr. said it best: "Earn your success based on the service to others, not at the expense of others."[2]

Not only does this delegate the wealth and success among your teammates and loved ones, it helps you find more relief for your self-discipline; it shifts the focus off of you. Rather than finding ways to make yourself feel better, you'll find more fulfillment in helping others.

We as humans are naturally selfish. Our society *encourages* us to be selfish, making it easy to spend money to get ourselves nice things and pretend like we have it all—this is a quick way to depression, my friend.

Many of you reading this might not be familiar with the football player, Robert Quinn. Back in 2013, he had one of the best seasons any defensive end has ever had. He broke the (at the time) St. Louis Rams franchise record for most sacks in a single season after he recorded his 18th sack, but his team finished 7-9, the last place in their division.

The person who he surpassed, Kevin Carter, who finished with 17 sacks in 1999, the same year that the St. Louis Rams won a Super Bowl.[3] Of the two, who do you think got more fulfillment?

Reaching personal goals and dreams *is* fulfilling—don't get me wrong. But what if we could bring others with us along the way? In my mind, that's even *more* rewarding!

You'll get more enjoyment out of life when you shift your focus from "*me* first" to "*others* first."

Here's an example: the next time that you're given a gift card, use part of it to reward someone else. Rather than getting temporary enjoyment from a cup of coffee for yourself, you'll receive *fulfillment* in doing something nice for a person that might have needed it more than you did.

Don't believe me? Think of it another way. Personal goals are temporary, but goals with others last forever. Kevin Carter's single-season sack record was broken, but guess what—*he* still has a Super Bowl ring on his finger.

Back when Robert Quinn broke the record, he mentioned that he would've traded it in for a long playoff run. He broke the record trying to get his team into the postseason.

Anyone can accomplish something for their own self-interest; it's those that bring others along for the ride that are remembered forever.

V. Implementing Self-Regulation

When you go to execute your goals, you're going to be faced with adversity; we all know this. None of us are able to dodge it. But how do you respond when it happens? Are you able to keep yourself in check?

For those of you who are unfamiliar with the term, "self-regulation" is when someone has the ability to keep their emotions, thoughts and feelings in check while they pursue a goal; it's how successful people are able to avoid becoming frazzled.

Self-regulation allows you to prevent things from worsening when you come into contact with an obstacle.

There will always be external factors—things we can't control—that set us back. However, we tend to do more damage than the initial obstacle by letting our emotions and thoughts run amuck; it's what leads to most people's impulsivity to give up, rather than fight through the pain.

If you're going to achieve your long-term goals, self-regulation is a must; it allows you to continue climbing that tree to the top. Staying positive helps you manage your emotional response to situations, such as dealing with an angry customer in order to retain their business.

Think about the best manager you've ever had. I'd be willing to bet that one of your favorite qualities about them was their ability to roll with the punches rather than fly off the handle; they kept their cool. That's self-regulation at its finest!

Even though "self" is in the word, your self-regulation plays a role in whether or not you'll receive external opportunities.

If you're striving for a promotion, but are unable to handle mistakes or setbacks with maturity, your boss will *never* give you a shot at becoming a manager.

Lucky for you, we've already learned the tricks to self-regulation: establishing firm goals—like we did in Chapter 2—then organizing those goals, cutting out distractions from our path and adapting to triggers whenever they rear their ugly heads. You've got this!

PHASE 3:

PERSISTENCE

Chapter 9

PERSEVERANCE

Fun story, here. I've actually had the idea to write this book for a few years now. After two to three years of sitting on it, I finally decided to put things into motion. I sent out my self-discipline survey to well-established professionals in my network, then started writing the framework for this book and gathering the responses from the surveys that were sent back to me.

After about two months of planning, I was finally ready to write the book. For several weeks, I'd sit down for an hour or two each day to work on it… Then the unthinkable happened.

One Thursday night, I had just finished writing two pages in the Goal-Setting Chapter. When I went to save my draft, my computer asked me if I'd like to replace the existing file.

"*Why, yes! I think I do!*" I thought to myself. So I clicked "replace and delete old file." That was a dumb move.

When I went to email the updated rough draft to myself—as I did every night after I finished writing—the rough draft was nowhere to be found. Not only had I accidentally erased the rough draft I was working on, I had somehow managed to erase the entire *folder* that I'd created for all the material for this book.

I lost *everything.*

The survey responses, the notes I made, the outline I'd created, the framework I'd pieced together. *All* of it.

I immediately called my dad—who works with computers and networks for a living—only to have him tell me there was no way to retrieve it. I can only imagine how hard it must have been for him to tell his son that he erased his own book.

I felt like fainting. I was so angry that I didn't know whether to throw my laptop against the wall or start ugly crying. I'm happy to report that I didn't end up doing either.

After a few hours went by, I remember telling myself one thing: what's done is done. As much as I hated it, there was no turning back—no way to reverse the mistake I'd made. Honestly, there was only one option if I ever wanted to complete my goal of writing this book: *start all over*.

As weird as it is to say now, it was a blessing in disguise. I gave myself three days to step away from the book and hit "reset" before starting new notes, a new draft and a new outline.

In a way, *you* are benefitting from my bone-headed mistake as well. The book you're reading right now is *way* better than the one I originally started.

The best part is that that story is now my testimony. If I wasn't already qualified to write about successful self-discipline before, I am *now*. I've lived it. I've had my own mistakes knock me on my butt and take away all of my progress, but I got right back up.

I don't tell you this story to pat myself on the back. In fact, it's pretty humiliating to admit that I willingly clicked on a tab that said "replace and delete." I'm telling you this because it proves something we all know in our hearts: there will be hurdles on your journey. Sometimes, those hurdles can be so high that you feel like you'll need to pole-vault to overcome them.

If we're using our Self-Discipline Tree metaphor here, then you could say I lost my grip the middle of the way up and fell down to the ground, hitting every tree branch on the way. How's *that* for an image?

But here's the beauty of it: with *perseverance*, you'll be able to overcome any setback you face and come back even stronger.

To kick off our Persistence Phase, we'll learn to overcome our failures and find inspiration to keep pushing to overcome something called "learned helplessness."

All of this starts by first understanding the different stages to pursuing your goal, and knowing when you should be ready to put your perseverance hat on and get to work. Let's start there!

I. The Stages of Goal Pursuit

In my mind, there's no better form of cinema than a good, old-fashioned superhero movie! It doesn't matter to me whether it's Marvel, DC or some other comic book publisher—they're all filled with action, suspense and some of the most awesome movie endings you'll ever see.

With that said, they all pretty much follow the same plot line, with a few exceptions.

When the movie starts, everything is roses and dandelions. Then—*uh-oh*—some form of evil villain comes along to take over the world. Superheroes can't allow that, so he or she steps in to save the day.

During their first encounter or two with the evil villain, our superhero usually gets their butts whooped, at which point they experience the lowest point of the entire movie; their girlfriend/boyfriend leaves them, someone important to them ends up dying in the crossfire—you get the idea.

In that moment, our superhero has two options: quit or go back and defeat the evil villain. He or she wouldn't be much of a hero if they chose the former, right?

Believe it or not, the typical path to our real-life goals and dreams aren't that different from a superhero movie's plot line. Where do you think the writers *got* those ideas?

You actually have more in common with superheroes than you realized!

Any time you pursue your goals, there are three initial stages that occur before the point where you must choose to persevere. These stages are:

1. The Initial Excitement— The thrill of the original idea.
2. The Hunt— Taking actionable steps towards the goal.
3. The Valley— The initial adversity and/or compounding failure.

Let's break each of these down a bit more.

First, we have the **initial excitement**. We all go through this whenever we have an idea that we like. If we come up with a goal that we're legitimately interested in, then the wheels start to churn and we get that first feeling of euphoria, along with a vision of seeing ourselves accomplishing that goal.

If the goal has legs, then we kick into the next stage: **the hunt**. This starts the very moment you take your first actionable step towards a goal. For example, if your goal is to lose weight, then going on your first run or buying a gym membership would begin your hunt. If you want to start a business, then the hunt may start when you draw up a business plan or buy the domain name for a site. You get the idea.

As long as things keep going well, we continue the hunt; we accomplish goals left and right; we're playing with house money. Then, we hit a bump — an initial point of adversity, which brings us to **the valley** stage.

Often times, whenever that first setback occurs, other hurdles and obstacles seemingly sprout up out of nowhere. It's like the old saying goes: "When it rains, it *pours.*"

I liken this to riding a roller coaster. You slowly-but-surely climb your way up to the highest point. *Click. Click. Click. Click.* Then all of a sudden, you're falling down a steep slope and the *real* ride begins.

Here's a friendly reminder for you: everyone fails. In fact, we rarely achieve any goal—small or large—without facing a few bumps along the way.

Whenever you start taking a beating, you'll find it tempting to give up. If you do, then the ride stops there. But if you're willing to stand up to those challenges and see them through, you'll start ascending once again. It's like one of my mentors always told me, "Life throws you a lot of curveballs. How you *respond* to that adversity will define your future."

From that, we can deduce one meaningful truth: you will only accomplish your goals if you persevere. There *is* no other way. Trust me, I've tried.

Without perseverance, you don't have self-discipline. If you can't handle a hitting slump and choose to hang up your cleats, then you'll never hit another home run in your life. Like the greatest hockey player of all time, Wayne Gretzky, used to say, "You miss 100-percent of the shots you don't take."

In order to prepare you for the valley stage, I've taken the liberty of listing a few common setbacks that people face when pursuing their goals. My hope is that by alerting you to these setbacks, it will help lessen the sting when—not if—they happen to you.

Common Setbacks:

1. **You start to question your ability:** *"Am I cut out for this?"*
2. **You begin to feel like an imposter:** *"Am I qualified to do this?"*
3. **You get distracted:** *"Should I pursue this other goal instead?"*
4. **You let negative thoughts fill your head:** *"I'll never succeed at this!"*
5. **You feel bad for yourself:** *"I'll never get what I want!"*
6. **You dwell on external factors that have set you back:** *"Why me?"*
7. **You let others dictate your goals for you:** *"They're right. I'm a nobody!"*[1]

II. Overcoming Learned Helplessness

We've all had those moments—countless moments—where we were the victim of repeated failure. It's like a snowball rolling down a hill—once one problem happens, they seem to pile up, don't they?

Whether we admit it or not, those compounding failures can start to take a toll on our psyche. Maybe you've endured a traumatic event that shook you to your core. Perhaps you've run into failure whenever you've tried to accomplish one distinct goal—such as a smoker who can't quit, even though they've tried.

Here's the hard truth: we *have* to push through. The responsibility doesn't fall on anyone but *you* to persevere. No one else can do it for you. People can encourage you and try to nudge you in the right direction; they can even pick you up and help dust you off, but you're the one that has to summon the courage to take that next step.

Here's another truth for you: whether you persevere or quit, you've made a definitive choice. Can you really accept knowing that you willingly gave up on your goals and dreams? I know I can't.

Should you choose to quit after several failed attempts, you could become the victim of what's called *learned helplessness.*

For those of you unfamiliar with the term, learned helplessness is when people develop toxic self-discipline traits after trying to achieve goals and failing.

If those toxic behavioral traits continue, the problem will only get worse. In fact, many psychologists believe learned helplessness to be one of the main causes of depression.[2]

The only way to prevent yourself from this slippery slope is to roll with the punches. Your past failures don't define you; it's how you *react* to those failures that reveals your true character.

III. Overcoming Failure

Mistakes and failures come in *many* different sizes. The big failures are the ones that take the wind out of our sails. The small failures are the ones that destroy our progress while we aren't paying attention.

The good news is that almost all failures are able to be overcome. You can get a head start on that by embracing the fact that failure *will* happen. No matter how successful you become or how many goals you achieve, you'll always face big and small failures; some are self-inflicted, others are external.

Let me give you an example. When I was a salesman in my previous career, being told "no" was just a part of the job. I made 60 to 80 calls a day, and almost all of them would either result in me leaving a voicemail or receiving some variation of "no."

"I can't talk about this right now." "Now is a bad time, call back later." "Your team sucks, call me when they're winning." "It's not in the budget right now." "We're moving to Zimbabwe." I pretty much heard it all.

But here's the thing about sales: you have to embrace the "no's" in order to get to a "yes," and let me tell you something—that one "yes" makes the ten or twenty previous "no's" worth it.

It's the same thing with undergoing failure and having the self-discipline to continue climbing towards the top of your tree. That one win, that one moment where you're standing at the very top of the tree, makes all of the failures, mistakes and hiccups worth it.

In a way, failure offers you a form of reassurance on your journey to fulfill a goal.

It's just like the superhero storyline I mentioned earlier. Our superhero doesn't just coast through the story until he or she defeats the main villain—that wouldn't be a very interesting (or realistic) story at all.

No, the protagonist faces *many* different obstacles along the way—most of which are caused by the very entity that they're trying to defeat.

I can promise you this: your story has many failures ahead of you, and that's a *good* thing. Failures teach you lessons; they motivate you; they give you an opportunity to pick yourself back up, dust yourself off and run faster than you ever have before.

IV. Finding the Drive to Push Through

Since we just used superhero movies as an example, how about we use it *one* more time?

One of my all-time favorites is *Batman Begins*. For those of you that haven't seen it, it's the story of how

Bruce Wayne, heir of Wayne Enterprises, became the hero we know and love as Batman—hence the name of the movie.

In the movie, Bruce has several moments where he loses faith and inspiration to keep going; his parents are killed by a street criminal, his city is on the brink of collapsing and his troubles take him all the way to a secret society known as the "League of Shadows."

But that's not even the worst of it. Bruce hits rock bottom when the movie's antagonist finds him at Wayne Manor (Bruce's house) and starts a fire to set his entire family's history ablaze.

Alfred, Bruce's resourceful butler, saves him and escorts him down the elevator to the Bat Cave *just* before the entire thing explodes.

Seeing the last of his parents' belongings going up in flames, Bruce starts to feel helpless and alone. At this point, he realizes that he's no match for the growing underground society of villains that he's paired up against.

Just as he's about to give up, Alfred reminds him of a pivotal question that Bruce's father used to ask him: "Why do we fall, Bruce?... So that we can pick ourselves back up."

That simple reminder of who he is and where he comes from was all Bruce needed to put the Batsuit on and face his enemies, even when the odds were stacked against him.

No matter how badly you want to achieve the goals that you've set, there will be times where inspiration fades; it comes and goes, generally around the time that you experience your biggest setback.

The good news is that motivation can be found to help you persist. No matter how many times you've failed at the goal that you're pursuing, keep your eyes peeled for extrinsic motivation (reward-driven behavior). Look for any source that can help you push through your adversity.

In the case of our Caped Crusader, he needed his trusty butler and closest confidant to remind him of who he was and why failure was a *good* thing.

My hope is that this book has produced a bit of extrinsic motivation for you already. Sometimes, all we need is a bit of clarity—a friendly reminder that life has a way of working itself out; all we need to do is keep pushing!

Work on perfecting your craft, not achieving your goal. If you do everything in your power to gain more knowledge and apply it to your work, then you'll achieve your goal without question.

Sadly, most people don't give themselves the chance. Studies show that 43% of people will give up on their goals within the *first month*.[3] Those numbers are only going to continue to rise due to the "I want it now" society that we live in. I've been guilty of it myself as well.

Many times, the motivation you need comes from the sources you use to hone your skills. For example, you could be reading a book pertaining to your career and read a tidbit of knowledge that shifts your thinking. You could be listening to a podcast and hear a statistic that blows your mind and regenerates the inspiration that you thought was lost.

Here's the truth: you don't need inspiration to keep working towards your goals. It's nice to have, sure, but not necessary.

Even when writing this book, there were several days where I couldn't see the light at the end of the tunnel. In those moments, all I could do was work on giving you the best product possible. Then, wouldn't you know it, the motivation kept on coming and the inspiration came back brighter than before.

As we'll see in the next chapter, whether or not you achieve your goals isn't the only thing that matters in achieving successful self-discipline; how you go about pursuing your goals is just as crucial.

If you want to reach an echelon that most people don't, you have to keep working towards your goals when most people won't. A majority of people won't push through when they lack inspiration and motivation. By simply working through those trying times, you've already set yourself apart from the rest!

These days, *The Lord of the Rings* is a household title. Whether you've ever seen the movies or read the books, you at least *know* of the franchise. It's one of the bestselling book series and the author, J.R.R. Tolkien, has been deemed by some experts to be the father of the fantasy book genre. But you might be shocked to find out that the books weren't well received when they first came out.

Critics targeted Tolkien specifically, claiming that his writing "lacked fiber" and was too "high-minded." Even fellow members of his and C.S. Lewis' *Inklings* Literary Club were tired of hearing about elves.

That criticism initially started in 1937 when *The Hobbit* was first released. Even with all of the negative feedback, J.R.R. went on to finish his *The Lord of the Rings* series, releasing the first two books in 1954 and the last one in 1955.[4]

Fast forward to today and the entire series, with *The Hobbit* included, are all listed as some of the best-selling books of all time.

The point? Success won't always come on the first try. If J.R.R. Tolkien had lacked self-discipline and passion, he may have let those negative reviews fill his head with doubt. Instead, he kept writing about "Middle Earth" and now, long after he's gone, his books continue to expand the boundaries of readers' imaginations.

I don't know what bumps you've hit along the way. I've no way of knowing the hurt you've felt when people shot down your dreams or goals. All I know is that you only have one choice if you want to succeed: *persevere*.

Chapter 10

REPUTATION

Can I get heavy for a second? What if you died before you completed the goals that you've set for yourself? What if you had ten long-term goals for your career and you only accomplished two of them before you retired? Would you consider yourself to be a failure in these scenarios?

The answer depends on one thing: whether or not you went about pursuing those goals the right way.

Whenever one phase of your life ends, there's only one thing that stays behind—your reputation. If you retire and all of your coworkers and employees remember you as a guy/girl that cut corners to get places, then you failed. But if they remember you as someone that tried to do right by everyone and worked your tail off to advance, then they'll remember you as a success.

Remember, self-discipline isn't results-based; it isn't even time-based. This means that even if you don't complete a goal within your certain window of time, you haven't failed. As long as you have the self-discipline to keep those legs churning, your goals are still within reach.

In football, a 4-yard run can either be impressive or disappointing, depending on the circumstance. If the running back is met by two defenders in the backfield and breaks a few tackles to gain four yards, it's impressive. But if his offensive line opened a huge hole for him and he trips over his own feet four yards downfield, it would be disappointing—as well as embarrassing and frustrating.

Those that see you work towards your goals every day don't look as hard at the results as you may think. A good boss isn't as impressed with a $20,000 sale as he or she is with your dedication to growing relationships with your clients and setting up in-person meetings. The sale is a result of the work you put in. Don't get me wrong, they'll still be impressed with the major cash feat. However, your reputation for hard work and self-discipline will validate what they already knew was in your future: success.

Let's focus on *that* aspect of it. We can't always control when we get the results we want. What we *can* always control is our legacy. The work you do or don't do each day will build that for you, whether you're conscious of it or not. I want to show you why your reputation is just as important as the success you experience in your life; it plays just as much of a factor into whether you achieve your goals as any other aspect of our Self-Discipline Tree.

I. Building Your Legacy

When one phase of your life ends, what do you want people to say about you? Is fame and fortune worth it if you trampled on everyone in your path to get there? Is it worth achieving your goals, turning back and seeing all of the people that you cut down to "succeed?" Do you *really* enjoy getting a first place medal if you found a shortcut to win the race? Let's break this down a bit further in order to provide some perspective.

When you retire, what do you want your coworkers to say about you and your work ethic? If you went about it the right way, they'll commend you for your willingness to work hard and your appreciation for those around you.

If you choose to take the easy route, people will remember you for juking the stats. Oh sure, they'll attend your retirement party because it's mandatory. But really, behind your back, they'll remember the truth: how you stepped on others, demeaned your coworkers and took credit for things that your subordinates did.

When your kids move out of the house, what do you want them to say about how you raised them? If you prioritized them, showed them love, taught them and even disciplined them, they'll remember you as a loving father/mother who did whatever they could to help them grow.

However, if your answer for everything was working late every night, screaming at them, leaving your spouse to do it all, or—even worse—*abandoning* your family, then they'll remember that too. Kids may sugarcoat their parents' faults while they grow up, but eventually, they'll accept the truth: you weren't a loving parent.

When you pass on from this life, what do you want people to say about how you lived and loved? If you kept a serve-first mindset and supported those whom you love, they'll remember you fondly; they'll always be reminded of little stories and moments where you showed your love, kindness or even steadfastness to those who you care about most.

But if you were selfish, you'll have a lightly-attended funeral. Very few people will remember you, and if they do, it won't be a positive thought that comes to their mind. If you were so caught up in your own self-interests your entire life, no one—including your own loved ones—will have a lasting impression of you: that's the cold, hard truth.

I don't know about you, but I want people to *smile* when they think of who I was and the encounters they had with me—however brief they may have been.

This book is focused on establishing successful self-discipline and traits that will help you establish your goals—but don't get it twisted. Your goals aren't the only thing that matters in this life. If you're *truly* using successful self-discipline, you're not allowed to belittle other people's goals to achieve your own. Even if you have the same goal as them, your objective is to help them achieve it for themselves one day.

For example, let's say you and one of your coworkers both want to become the Vice President (VP) of Marketing at your company. You should both work hard to beat the other one out, that's the healthy competition that we talked about in our Execution Chapter.

If *they* end up getting the VP position, then you *must* respect the outcome. Be ticked off, if you want, but compounding negative thoughts only lead to one place: failure.

If *you* get the VP position, then your objective becomes clear: use your platform to help your coworker succeed. Find other opportunities for them. Give them more responsibility. Help them find a VP position at another company in order to help them excel in their career and achieve *their* long-term goals. You see how successful self-discipline can lead to building your legacy?

In my life, I've come across some people with *amazing* reputations: I know pastors that are selfless; I know CEOs whose number one passion is helping college kids get their start in their career; I've met people who have a past filled with tragedies that they then used those as a testimony to help others. I've tried to soak up as much as I can from these types of people.

Here's the one constant I've found: they don't focus on their legacy—they focus on helping others in any way that they can. They climb their tree to the top, and while looking down at the people on the ground, say, "Come on up, guys! It's fun! You can do it, too!"

Being a Christian, I believe that there is an even *better* life for us after this one, but once we pass on, there's only one thing left of us on Earth: our legacy. If we care for others and serve them to the best of our abilities, our legacy can extend down *many* generations after we're gone. How cool is that?!

II. Protecting Your Personal Brand

Do you have the courage to be honest, even when you know it will cast aspersion against you? Are you humble enough to accept that everyone on your team or at your job has something to offer?

Protecting your personal brand is important, but not at the expense of other people. Successful self-discipline is about doing what's right, even if it means fessing up to your mistakes or failures.

I'll give you an example. Back when I got my start working for the Arizona Coyotes as a ticket sales representative, our sales management had a very organized and analytical approach to sales; they monitored call numbers and call times very closely. More quality calls equals more sales!

Since they were monitoring call numbers so diligently, it held me (and others at my job) accountable for our work; that was ideal, considering most of the sales reps were either fresh out of college or only two to three years removed from it.

One day, I found out that there was a phone number that some ticket sales representatives were calling to inflate their call numbers and talk time. It was a harmless phone number that you could call and it would play some music for as long as you wanted it to.

Rather than doing the smart and ethical thing, I took the irresponsible route and partook in calling this number whenever my call time or call count was lower than it needed to be.

Then, one day, our VP of Sales walked onto the sales floor *fuming*. He informed us all that he caught wind of some ticket sales reps calling that phone number. He told us that he was having the sales managers go through all our calls from the last 10 days, and that anyone who called the number from their desk phone would be fired.

As you can imagine, I was horrified. Here my career had barely begun and I was already caught up in what would be—thankfully—the most unethical thing I'd do in my sales career.

I had a decision to make: shrug my shoulders and act like I didn't know what number he was referring to or fess up. The way I saw it, I was likely going to get canned anyways—might as well have some fiber of integrity and fess up to it.

At the end of my shift, I walked into our VP's office with my legs shaking. I closed the door behind me and admitted that I had called the phone number several times and apologized for it. Thankfully, he didn't ask me to rat out who I'd gotten the number from or anyone else I knew that was using it.

To my surprise, the VP thanked me for confessing. Not only did he let me keep my position, but it led to a *very* healthy conversation about the pressures we were feeling as salesmen and saleswomen. It started an hour-long brainstorming session between him and I about how we could add more helpful accountability practices for the entire staff.

If I could go back in time, I might choke myself out with the cord from my desk phone for ever calling that number. But this story is a great example of why integrity is crucial to any goal we set out to accomplish.

There are two key factors to integrity: humility and honesty. We often think that, in the most crucial moments, those two characteristics are our worst enemy—that they'll expose our faults and diminish our worth in the eyes of others. It's quite the opposite. I'd go so far as to say that they're the two most important tools to have when you're backed into a corner.

It's all about doing what's right for yourself and your team, family, company, etc. If I hadn't confessed to calling that phone number, I would've been doing all my coworkers a disservice—especially the ones that never called that number and chose to call *actual* clients instead.

I promise you, there is always a reward waiting on the other side of integrity. I thought for sure that I was getting fired as soon as I confessed. I envisioned our VP of Sales throwing his hot coffee in my face as he called for security to take me away.

Instead, he *commended* me. That one conversation kick-started a great business relationship between him and I. Even though I messed up, my confession showed him that he could trust me.

Only a year or two later, that mentor would help me land an amazing position with the Tampa Bay Buccaneers. My new boss would eventually tell me what my mentor said to convince him to hire me: "Zach's a guy that you can always trust."

To be fair, the reward of integrity isn't always as grand; sometimes it's just peace of mind knowing that you did the right thing. But here's another thing about honesty and humility: they are two of your greatest teachers. I never did anything like that again in my career, and I never will. Integrity can do the same for you, too.

III. Protecting Your Online Image

The digital world is changing our lives more and more each day, with more information out there on the internet about each of us than ever before. The crazy part is that most of us *choose* to place that information on the internet without realizing it. We sign up for social media profiles on many different platforms (Facebook, Twitter, etc.), fill out our profiles, post intimate details about our lives and so on.

I don't say that to scare you. I personally am not against social media. As I've mentioned in this book, it can be a beautiful way to connect people—but there's no denying the negative consequences it can have as well, which I've *also* mentioned in previous chapters.

One of the *worst* consequences of social media is how it can tarnish your personal brand. Whether you like it or not, people make different opinions and judgements on you based on what you put out there.

If you choose to put self-damaging images of you partying and acting immaturely, it *will* come back to bite you; it can ruin your path to achieving your goals before you even get started. You can do *everything* else right, but your choice to negatively personify yourself on social media can cut down your Self-Discipline Tree *as* you're climbing it.

Don't believe me? Here's a stat for you, then. CareerBuilder once did a survey proving that over 70-percent of employers use social media as a tool for their background screening process.[1] That survey was back in 2017, so you can bet that number has climbed even *more* since then. If you've been wondering why you didn't hear back from any employers you've reached out to about a position, your social media may have scared them off.

A few years ago, I had a colleague that was looking to take the next step in his career by becoming a Sales Manager. Our company didn't have any openings, so he took initiative and started to apply for manager positions with other companies.

Let me tell you, the dude had almost *every* qualification in the book: years of experience, leadership skills, impressive sales numbers, hard work ethic, great communication skills and a tremendous personality. He was *ready* to be a manager—no doubt about it.

Yet after months of applying for managerial roles, he wasn't getting far with many employers.

After not hearing back from a company that he was referred to by a client, he asked his connection to find out anything they could as to why they never ended up reaching out to him.

The answer? The employer had looked at my colleague's Facebook page and saw several political posts that could be seen as offensive by others.

Now, does that mean that every employer that turned him down did so for the same reason? Of course not—there could be other factors at play. But I'd be willing to bet they weren't the only employer that saw those posts.

I'm not telling you that you can't ever express yourself on social media. I'm not saying that you have to go through and delete every photo you've ever posted.

What I *am* telling you is to consider how those posts and photos are affecting your personal brand. Casting negative aspersions on yourself can naturally generate external factors that will diminish your goals.

Take the time to go through all of your social media accounts and perform a complete audit of your content. Go through every photo and post and ask yourself,

"Would an employer or one of my mentors approve of this?" If not, then delete it.

Treat your social media like a business. Companies are prioritizing public relations and branding more than ever before—you should do the same. By taking just a little bit of time to clean the slate, you could be avoiding *major* hurdles down the line.

IV. Fruit of the Holy Spirit

I could sit here and tell you all of the attributes that we should have as moral men and women who are looking to achieve our goals, but truth be told, someone else has beaten me to it. His name was Paul; Paul the Apostle, to be exact. Quite frankly, he explained it better than I ever could!

Any time I'm looking for direction, I turn to one book: the *Holy Bible*. For believers like myself, it's a tremendous way to gain perspective and understanding. Plus, it helps remind us of the big picture: there's more to life than our own goals and desires.

In the book of Galatians, Paul outlined what he referred to as the "fruit of the Holy Spirit." These are different qualities that believers of the Spirit should exude in order to live a fulfilling and—pardon my pun—"fruitful" life the way God intended.

Even if you aren't religious, the fruit of the Spirit can help you strive for excellence in the way you pursue your goals.

Galatians 5:22-23 says:

"But the fruit of the Spirit is love, joy, peace, patience, kindness, goodness, faithfulness, gentleness, and self-control. Against such things there is no law."[2]

Did you catch all of those? Love. Joy. Peace. Patience. Kindness. Goodness. Faithfulness. Gentleness. Self-Control. If we're being honest, those can be some of the *hardest* qualities to maintain. If we aren't careful, we'll skim over them all without taking in the true power they can offer. I won't let that happen! Let's break each of them down a bit further.

LOVE - Some people in our lives are easy to love. Others... not so much. If we're going to truthfully see the beauty in life and uplift others with us as we accomplish our goals, we have to love them with all our might, just as God does.

JOY - Joy is more than happiness. Joy is the feeling of ultimate pleasure and, more importantly, thankfulness. Those that are thankful for what they *currently* have, not what they hope to gain in the future, are the only ones in this life that are truly joyous.

PEACE - Can you stand firm when the going gets rough? Peace is vital to self-discipline and building a lasting legacy. It allows you the ability to weather the storm and come out unscathed.

PATIENCE - Can you follow the path you've set out on, even when there's adversity heading your way? True patience is shown by those that follow God's commands and trust the process *passionately*. Paul was also referencing the ability to have patience with others, even when they cross us.

KINDNESS - By the world's standards, kindness is anyone that can muster up a smile. By the Bible's standards, true kindness is exuded by treating others how you wish to be treated. It even calls us to turn the other cheek at times—which can be a tough pill to swallow, I'll admit!

GOODNESS - Goodness is unselfish. Goodness has no bias. Goodness is shown through our actions; it calls us to go above and beyond for others. But here's the kicker: goodness is all about the intent behind it. When we act in the best interests of others, we should do so without any selfish implications.

FAITHFULNESS - Are you willing to stick it out and trust others, even after they've wronged you? Faithfulness is about believing; believing in another person's potential; believing that your goals are yours for the taking, even when they don't seem close. People remember those that are faithful to them, but they're quick to forget those that aren't.

GENTLENESS - What's the use of accomplishing your goals if you don't help others to accomplish *theirs*? I promise you, it's not as rewarding. Jesus had all the reason in the world to show superiority over mankind, but he never did. He stayed humble and gentle—why should we do any less?

SELF-CONTROL - Do you have the ability to avoid the temptation to quit or veer from your path? The Bible calls for more than the ability to control ourselves; it calls for us to give up our selfish desires and let Him lead the way. To be clear, that doesn't mean you should never pursue a goal that you want. Just make sure that your ideals and God's plan for the goal goes hand-in-hand.

I grew up in the church, so I first learned the fruit of the Spirit in Sunday school. I've heard that verse recited countless times since then, but I can't recall ever hearing the last verse, verse 26, being mentioned. I would argue it has just as important of a message as the fruit of the Spirit.

Galatians 5:26 reads:

"Let us not become conceited, provoking, and envying each other."

If we're all being honest, we catch ourselves becoming those three things *a lot*. If we let them, they can tarnish our entire reputation *and* the self-discipline we need to chase our goals.

Make a promise to yourself right here and now: any time you find yourself filling your head with pride, becoming jealous or deliberately trying to anger someone else—nip it in the bud. These are time-wasting qualities that will only drag you down. Instead, focus on positive thoughts. Give thanks for the people and things you *do* have in your life. That will quickly get your head back into focus!

Chapter 11

ACCOUNTABILITY

Back when I worked as a Footwear Associate for Dick's Sporting Goods, I didn't have a care in the world. I was 18 years old, lived with my parents and had *zero* responsibility for anything or anyone else out there... and it showed.

Back then, I saw my job as more of a hangout spot than an actual means of making money—terrible, I know.

Don't get me wrong, I did everything that was expected of me: I was friendly with customers; I'd help them try on shoes and give my professional opinion whenever they asked for it; I'd stock the shelves and clean the bathrooms at night, but I wasn't one to go above and beyond.

At the time, Dick's Sporting Goods had this program that they referred to as "S.W.E.E.T." It stood for "Socks

With Each and Every Transaction." As the name would imply, the goal of it was for footwear associates—such as myself—to have as many customers purchase a pair of socks (or 3-pack or 6-pack) with any pair of shoes that they were planning on buying.

Looking back, it was an *ingenious* program. Not only would it drive more sales for the company, but it caused employees to be more intentional when talking to customers.

They introduced the "S.W.E.E.T." program *long* before I got hired. By the time I came around, it was only mentioned in signage. I briefly remember a coworker telling me about it in passing, but it fell on deaf ears.

Being the immature 18 year old that I was, I took the program literally. I'd think to myself, *"Why do I care if a customer buys socks? What is so special about these socks? Why does my manager keep going on about socks?"* Needless to say, I never paid it much attention.

About six months after I started, we got a new store manager. One of the first things he did was take the time to meet with each of us individually to get to know us better.

When my turn came around, the new manager spent a few minutes making small talk with me, then ended our meeting with one sentence: "You seem like a great kid, and you do a great job, but I need to see your 'S.W.E.E.T.' numbers improve."

Wait… WHAT? I remember thinking to myself, *"You guys actually CARE about that thing? I thought that was just something we talked about during our morning huddles to fill the time."*

My mind was *blown*. As soon as I found out my managers were actually watching my sales numbers, my entire attitude changed.

Suddenly, I started mentioning socks with every customer and—wouldn't you believe it—I began selling more socks! I was even selling socks to the customers that *didn't* buy shoes. What can I say? I was making the St. Peters, Missouri store *rain* in socks.

About a month after our initial meeting, the store manager came up to me, smiled, and said, "I wish all changes were that easy to make!" and walked away.

So what changed for me? How did I go from not caring about a corporate selling incentive to talking about socks more than I ever had in my 18 years of existence?

The answer is simple: accountability. Someone was holding me responsible for the output I produced in my job. Rather than just mentioning it in passing, my new boss explained the importance of it and held me to a higher standard.

To truly unlock the power of accountability, we need to understand where and how we can summon it. Let's find out where accountability comes from, so that we can capitalize on it to develop successful self-discipline.

I. The Sources of Accountability

Accountability is a powerful tool. Trust me, if it can drive a careless teenager to sell socks, it can help you achieve any goals you set for yourself; it helps you generate inspiration and can breed motivation when the going gets tough.

The best part? Accountability can be found all over the place. It's important to know where we can find the right *kind* of accountability so that we can use it to our advantage.

If we know where to find it, then we can seek it out. We can rely on it when our fuel level gauge is reading "E." While accountability doesn't always come from within, we can still use it as a building block for self-discipline.

There are three prominent sources that you can gain accountability from: yourself, others and content. Let's take a dive into all three.

Source #1: Personal Accountability

Anytime you find yourself looking around for help, you should first take the time to look *within*. The truth is that we as individuals have *much* more mental strength than we think; some people just choose not to use it.

Remember when we talked about willpower being a muscle? Well, just like physical muscles, there are those out there who prefer not to exercise it at all, rather than push it to its limits.

Personal accountability is crucial to your success, and not just for the big, difficult choices. You'll have to wake yourself up each day. You'll have to commit to sitting down and writing that book each day. You'll have to convince yourself to not eat that jelly-filled donut that's sitting in the pantry.

But what it really comes down to is this: can you be a self-starter? Some of you already are. Others of you will have to learn the tricks of the trade. There is no shame in admitting that!

Being a self-starter makes working towards your goals each day become second nature. At first, you'll have to make conscious decisions that are pivotal to your goals. But after performing them consistently for a while, those conscious tasks suddenly become subconscious. In other words—you start to do them without realizing it!

I'll give you an example. Being a salesman or saleswoman is no easy gig. With that said, it's *much* easier to be productive when you're on a busy sales floor: the phones are ringing; your colleagues are making sales; managers are hopping from meeting to meeting; the buzz of others around you naturally encourages you to do the same.

But what if that sales floor was taken from you? What if you had to, for example, work from home instead? Would you still find the motivation within yourself? Would you still be able to make 80 calls a day, schedule appointments and continuously work/learn to perfect your craft?

Personal accountability can help you push through; it drives you to ignore external factors and work on the tasks at hand. It becomes like a personal trainer in your head, constantly pushing you and urging you to keep going.

So how do we get to that point? How can you begin to hold yourself more personally accountable and become a self-starter? By starting with your weaknesses.

Think back to the different aspects of self-discipline that we've covered in this book. Which of them have you suffered with the most? Which of them feel like a foreign concept to you?

Do you see the importance of those aspects now? Do you understand how you can use them to better yourself? Do your goals rely on you fixing those weaknesses? The answer to that last question is "yes"—just helping you out!

The best way to generate some personal accountability is by establishing goal checkpoints. The good news is that you already did that when you created short-term goals in our Goal-Setting Chapter. Now it's just a matter of putting them into action!

Take some time each day to look at your list of goals and assess where you're at. Sprinkle in a few reminders to keep focused on your short-term and long-term goals; that alone will give you the inspiration and accountability you need to push through!

I used this exact trick when writing this book. When I started writing the framework for the book, I envisioned a design for the cover art of the book. So, to inspire myself, I created a rough draft of that cover art and placed it on the background of my phone so that I'd look at it multiple times a day.

Source #2: Accountability From Others

Just like the great Bill Withers sang in his song *Lean on Me*, "We all need somebody to lean on." Accountability breeds the best results 100-percent of the time; even some of the most influential people in history knew that.

C. S. Lewis and J. R. R. Tolkien are the most prevalent example of this. Both of these men were professors at the prestigious University of Oxford in England. As most of us well know, they would go on to write some of the most popular and incredible fantasy stories of all time. Lewis being the author of *The Chronicles of Narnia* and Tolkien being the author of *The Hobbit* and *The Lord of the Rings*.

But what most of us don't realize is that some of their greatest books are the byproducts of *years* of accountability from like-minded friends and colleagues.

Lewis and Tolkien's weekly meetings at the local pub would eventually turn into a group known as "The Inklings," a group of 19 men that would meet to critique and uplift each other's literature pieces. As I understand it, this group met late every Thursday night for almost *twenty* years.

Different guys would bring along different pieces; they'd read poems, papers, letters and the like. As I mentioned earlier in this book, Tolkien would bring along different chapters of *The Lord of the Rings* as he wrote them.

While history doesn't tell us how much of a role "The Inklings" played in changing the story and format of these famous stories, I have to imagine the role that they played was fairly significant. At the very least, they encouraged Lewis and Tolkien to continue writing and perfecting their craft.

C. S. Lewis said as much when he was documented as saying that, "What I owe them all (the Inklings) is incalculable."

But there's a catch to finding accountability from others—you have to find like-minded people. The Inklings didn't just thrive and meet for twenty years because they were all men that got along— they each had a deeper personal connection with many similarities and common interests. They were all Christian men, they were all passionate about literature, most of them were scholars, they were all friends and many of them served in the British Army during World War I (C. S. Lewis and J. R. R. Tolkien both did).[1]

Did you catch it when I said the group consisted of 19 men? That's a pretty random number, but I guarantee you it was strategic. The only way anyone was getting into that group was if they shared a good majority of the morals and interests that the rest of the group had.

While that might seem harsh, it helped the group remain productive. Each of them legitimately cared about the stories that their pals were creating; that led to insight and constructive critiquing.

If you're going to harness the power of receiving accountability from others, make sure to be *intentional*. Find people that can share like-minded goals and interests—create your version of an Inklings group! Invite people that can provide you with accountability as you climb your Self-Discipline Tree, and vice versa!

I'll warn you ahead of time—these people aren't easy to find. You can't just build an Inklings group overnight. Instead, start by finding *one* person to meet with at a physical location (such as a coffee shop, restaurant, etc.) once a week to talk about life, your goals and create action towards your dreams; it will help you reengage with your vision and push you to be more productive. We'll talk about this a bit more in-depth when we cover how to find a support system in the next segment.

Source #3: Accountability From Content

Whether you like it or not, content plays a huge role in our lives these days. You can either let that scare you, or embrace it and take advantage of it.

You might not realize it, but the content that you take in is either holding you accountable to your goals or pushing you away from them. In other words—it's either making you productive or unproductive.

Don't believe me? Look at the last YouTube video you watched. Does that have anything to do with the goals you listed in our Goal-Setting Chapter? What is the last show you watched? I'd be willing to bet it isn't encouraging you to get off the couch and achieve a small win.

Instead, we need to hold ourselves more accountable to the content we digest so that *it* can provide *us* with more accountability and motivation.

Instead of listening to podcasts that are literally filling your ears with nonsense for one to two hours, listen to podcasts on the subject that your goals are tied into.

Rather than watching gym fail videos on YouTube for 30 minutes nonstop, watch videos that apply to the business you hope to build.

I'll give you an example. Readers, I'd like to introduce you to "Rick." Rick is interested in starting his own life-coaching business one day.

To create more accountability for himself, he's decided to watch YouTube videos that help him learn about search engine optimization for the website he wants to create. To make time for them, he's giving up the time he'd normally spend watching the latest music videos from his favorite artists.

While on his daily run, he's also chosen to listen to a podcast on life-hacking, budgeting, wellness and other topics that he wants to incorporate into his life-coaching business model one day.

You get the idea. By choosing to replace a few time-wasting forms of content, Rick is creating more accountability towards his future business. At the same time, he's growing his knowledge and learning how to manage his time more effectively—both of which will come in handy down the line!

II. Finding a Support System

Throughout this book, I've mentioned a few golden nuggets of wisdom that one of my dearest mentors shared with me about the subject of self-discipline. Well, I saved the best one for last!

One of the things he advocates most is finding a strong support system. He once told me that, "Accountability is the gauge of our degree of self-discipline." In other words, how intentional or unintentional you are with creating accountability for yourself has a direct reflection on how much self-discipline you have.

As I mentioned in the subhead about finding accountability from others, the support system you build *has* to be like-minded.

That's not to say that you have to be identical all the way around. A bit of contrast is a good thing; it gives you a different perspective. Otherwise, you might as well talk to your reflection in the mirror—it would be just as productive.

Just like C. S. Lewis and J. R. R. Tolkien, your support system can often be traced back to one or two people.

What started out as a weekly get-together every Monday morning to have a beer—yes, you read that correctly—eventually turned into a Thursday night focus group of strong, educated Christian men. At the heart of it all was a connection and friendship they all shared. That friendship among 19 different men was kick-started by a friendship between *two* men—Lewis and Tolkien. They were the nucleus.

I don't mean to get sappy here, but the nucleus to my support system has always been—and always will be—my wife, Bre. She helps me compensate for my weaknesses. She's the very reason that this book—and all of my other accomplishments—came to fruition.

We've all spent a fair bit of time analyzing our personal weaknesses. Find yourself a spouse that turns those weaknesses into a strength.

I have a very laid-back mindset. At times, that can be a good thing. For instance, I believe that my laid-back mentality helps me cope with stress better than most people. However, that same mentality can be a *huge* weakness when it comes to preparing, planning and even accomplishing things that aren't at the forefront of my mind.

Fortunately for me, my wife is always thinking ten steps ahead. It isn't uncommon for her and her entire family to be planning out the details of next year's family vacation *while* we're sitting on the beach for *that* year's vacation.

As if that wasn't helpful enough, she also has a "Go-Go-Go" mindset, helping her knock tasks out left and right. I have to admit, it's quite a spectacle to behold!

But the key to any significant friendship, and I'm sure you've heard this before, is communication. Without proper communication, the entire support system can quickly become disconnected.

If you aren't expressing your opinion and giving feedback, then the other person will make assumptions about what you're thinking. More often than not, those assumptions aren't positive—our heads tend to go to the darkest of places, don't they?

Communicate your goals with your closest confidants. For me, that's my wife. For you, it might be someone else; maybe it's one of your siblings; maybe it's one of your mentors. Whoever it is, tell them about your dreams and speak those goals into existence; the second you do, you've started putting accountability in motion. Now that the nucleus of your support system knows your short-term and long-term goals, they can keep you in check. Don't forget to do the same for them and *their* goals!

III. Finding Mentorship

Derek Redmond had it made in the shade. Even despite his injury-riddled career, the British track star was ready to take the world by storm at the 1992 Olympics in Barcelona. The media was all but ready to embrace his Cinderella story after he won a Gold medal.

He had a great first round, and all seemed right with the world. However, during the semi-final, things turned quickly. Redmond got off to a great start which, even *he* admits, was unusual. His reaction to the pistol would allow him to pace himself around the bend and still have plenty of energy in case he needed to push himself closer to the line.

Just as he rounded the bend, he felt a *"pop."* He tore his hamstring and immediately fell to the ground in agonizing pain.

This could have been the end to his career. If he continued to lay there, he'd be remembered as the guy that never got up; he wasn't about to let that happen.

Redmond sat on the ground for no longer than three seconds before he pushed off the medical team that had stormed to tend to him, climbed up to his feet, then hopped on one foot the rest of the way. He was determined to get to the finish line.

Both the spectators at the stadium and viewers at home watched in amazement as Redmond hobbled and hopped, making his way around the second bend. About 34 seconds later (by my count), Derek's father, Jim Redmond, rushed to his son's side and clutched Derek in his arms. The two of them exchanged a few words, then Jim walked with his son all the way to the finish line, shooing off any staff member that tried to stop them.

When asked about that moment in an interview with *The Australian* in 2017, Jim Redmond said: "When I got there (on the track), he insisted on finishing the race. So I said to him: 'We started your career together and we will finish it together.'"[3]

Derek was brave enough to get back up when most others would've thrown in the towel. An external factor—his injury—may have taken his hopes of the Gold medal, but he wouldn't let it take away his goal of finishing. That decision didn't just come from his own determination—it came from how he was raised. It came from the never-say-die attitude he'd been taught as a child. It came from his father, Jim—the most important mentor in his life.

I cannot overstress the importance of finding strong mentors. Whenever I look back at the best decisions I've made in my personal life and career, I notice one thing: it wasn't *me* that made those decisions—not really.

Any smart career move I've made or personal growth I've experienced can be traced back to the advice I was given by a mentor.

Back when I made the jump from my career as an Account Executive with the Tampa Bay Buccaneers to becoming a full-time writer, I kept going back to one quote from Mark Twain that my dad used to always tell me: "Find a job you enjoy doing, and you will never work a day in your life."[2]

In the end, that decision to take a leap of faith in my career was easier than it should have been. Why? Because I had mentors that gave me confidence to pursue it. Every single one of them gave me the green light—my wife included.

The benefits of finding mentors are plentiful. First, they'll always be a voice of reason. If we're being honest, we all make mistakes and pursue goals that we shouldn't. Mentors will give you the honest opinion that others won't. While everyone else shrugs their shoulders and says "Sure, go for it," your mentors will give you concrete explanations as to why you should or shouldn't take action towards a goal. That's worth its weight in gold!

Mentors can also help you gain reassurance as you attempt to climb to the top of your Self-Discipline Tree. In the moments when you start to doubt your abilities, strengths or self-worth, your mentors will straighten you out; they'll be the ones to push you—even *shove* you, if that's what it takes—to ensure that you reach the top of your tree. The truth is, even the most self-disciplined people have self-doubt at times; their mentors and support system are what helps them to refocus.

But here's the most valuable element of great mentors: they're willing to walk down that path with you. Imagine how much easier it'd be to reach the top of your Self-Discipline Tree if you had other people climbing it with you, encouraging you and challenging you the whole way up. How much more confidence would you have in your long-term goals if your mentors were there pushing you to new heights? Instead of you settling for the short-term goals and small goals you've achieved, they'll remind you to keep your eyes on the prize and shoot for those big goals instead—*that's* true mentorship.

Here's my challenge to you: don't just settle for one great mentor. There are *several* awesome mentors out there for you to find. The mixture of their knowledge and experiences can transform your life for the better; they'll help you mature and grow as you work to achieve both your short-term and long-term goals.

In *Star Wars*, Luke Skywalker didn't just have one mentor, he had several! Obi-Wan Kenobi was his original mentor, showing him the ways of the force and challenging him to fulfill his destiny. Down the line, Luke also finds mentorship from Jedi Master Yoda, who helped Luke refine his Jedi skills and (spoiler alert!) put himself in a position to—one day—defeat Darth Vader. You could even make the debate that Han Solo was a mentor to Luke in his own, unique way.

Having multiple mentors can ensure that you're making the right decisions and actions; you can listen to the voice of several, rather than the voice of one. Even your mentors can make a bad call, but if more of them are encouraging you to take action in one way, you'll feel more confident that you're making the right choice.

So where do you go to find mentors? That answer depends on the *type* of mentor you're looking for. That will take a bit of effort and intention on your part.

Start by assessing your current list of mentors. What areas of your life are they helping you mature and grow in? How are they helping you improve?

Next, identify areas of your life where you *don't* currently have strong mentors. Where can you go to find the guidance you need? Look for events and locations where that area of your life is at the forefront.

For example, if you're looking for business mentors, look at the leadership in your company; attend networking events; go to seminars and trade shows in the industry you're interested in; use social media to find mentors who prioritize helping people above making sales or pushing their own products.

If you want mentors to help you with exercise and fitness, sign up for a free trial with a trainer; strike up a conversation with the guy/girl at your gym that you want to look like; go to fitness expos and connect with experts online.

Those of you looking for mentors on your faith and family, look at the leadership in your church; ask your pastor to grab coffee with you; join a small group; read devotions.

Finding great mentors takes action on your part. After all, your ears have to be open to the advice they give. Finding a mentor who gives out a bit of tough love from time to time is always nice too. Often times, the things we *don't* want to hear are the instructions or tidbits of advice that we *need* to hear the most.

Although "self" is in the word, your self-discipline is an exact representation of the connections, mentors and loved ones that you surround yourself with. If you don't have means of accountability, you'll never hold yourself to a higher standard.

Successful self-discipline comes from the inspiration that you conjure up within yourself. However, that inspiration (or lack thereof) is a replication of the quality of your support system. Find a strong support system to boost the level of accountability in your life. But remember, you have just as much to offer them, as they have to offer you!

CONCLUSION

All three phases of this book—Preparation, Production and Perseverance—depend on you to take action. Mentors and loved ones can encourage you and challenge you to improve, but *you're* the one who has to take the first step.

These phases are constructive on their own, but when you combine them—that's when you'll experience true, unparalleled *success*.

Do you know what the true definition of "success" is? According to Oxford Languages, success is "the accomplishment of an aim or purpose."[1]

Did you catch that last part?

Success isn't just accomplishing a goal for the sake of accomplishing something; it's when you've executed a goal for a reason. There is *intent* behind success. Success differs from person to person though, so it's important to find out what "success" truly means to you.

Let's Review

After reading this book, you now know how to put *intention* into any goal you want in your personal or professional life. You've found out how to find your gift: by staying AWAKE (Aware, Willing, Available, Knowledgeable and Excited). You understand the roles that both inspiration (internal) and motivation (external) play in the goals that you set out to achieve. And you understand how self-awareness fuels self-discipline.

When it comes to *goal-setting*, you now have the tools to list out all of your goals. You can establish a defining point. You can self-audit. To set yourself up for success, you have to flesh out your long term goals first, then institute short-term goals that fall in line with each of them.

Remember: long-term goals aren't achievable without short-term goals. Make sure those short-term goals are **SMART** (Specific, Measurable, Achievable, Relevant and Timely). Use your **Personal Priority List** to get all of your goals and dreams on paper, then prioritize them as you so choose.

Once you have those goals listed out, you need to *organize* them. In our Organization Chapter, we learned how important time management is to self-discipline. It can even help you weather the storm when handling multiple responsibilities. Take the time to switch your mindset from achieving *work-life balance* to achieving *life-work balance*. Use that Personal Priority List to see which aspects of your life are most important to you.

Lastly, you need to use the **Bing-Goal Board** to cross off all your goals as you achieve them, then *reward* yourself for doing so. The reward is vitally important. As we discussed, a habit loop can't be created without following this exact cadence: cue, routine and reward. We're here to create a habit loop for accomplishing goals!

The most overlooked aspect to accomplishing any goal is *cleansing*. In our Cleansing Chapter, we learned about the different negative influences that should be deleted from our lives. We learned how to balance out the distractions of social media and time-wasting apps, as well as two exercises for taking back control of them—our Zero-Notification exercise and our Purge-and-Reassess exercise.

You're now fully aware of the temptations that you'll face as you work your way to the top of your Self-Discipline Tree—the temptation to quit, to doubt, and to pursue other goals. To adjust your habits and jump over your biggest hurdles, you can cleanse by replacing. Instead of picking up your phone to scroll, pick up a book. Instead of streaming movies, listen to audiobooks.

Once you've prepared and organized your goals, it's time to produce! If you focus on improving your exercise routine and nutrition, you can build keystone habits that will carry over into other aspects of your life; these will set you up for success as you start climbing your tree. Exercise is much easier when you plan your workouts and understand the "why" behind the plan that you're following. What's just as important is maintaining a positive outlook on your workouts. You don't *have* to work out, you *get* to work out. You *get* the chance to improve yourself physically and mentally.

Nutrition is no different. To see better results in your nutrition, you have to be intentional. You have to come up with a plan (or find a plan) that works for your daily routine. Understanding the "why" behind your eating habits can help you get to the root of the problem—if there *is* a problem.

When all else fails, schedule your meals. Give yourself specific time slots to consume all your calories for the day. Developing a habit of scheduling your meals will help you learn how to schedule other areas of your life as you pursue your goals.

Of course, it's just as important to maintain well-being while you're producing results; the power of optimism can't be matched. Remember, optimism isn't about *being happy all the time*, it's about *being hopeful about what lies ahead* of you. Think of it this way: if you don't keep your head up as you run towards your goals, you're bound to run into an obstacle eventually.

To create true mental self-discipline, you have to focus on consistently producing optimism while prioritizing integrity, respectfulness, trust, self-esteem, willpower and focus. All of these characteristics are easy to maintain as long as you make time to *meditate*. True meditation is about giving yourself time to prepare and adjust for what lies ahead. Write out your daily routine, then find a few minutes here and there to meditate. Take some time to say a quick prayer. Take a few deep breaths. Visualize the rest of your day.

To keep consistent well-being as you pursue your goals, you must also focus on your faith. Remember the question my pastor challenged us with: "If your physical nature reflected the nourishment of your spiritual nature, would we immediately send you to the hospital?"

Having faith helps you keep perspective of your life. You don't have to do this alone. You *shouldn't* do this alone. Allowing God to take the wheel on your life will free you of stress from external factors. It will give you confidence, even in the most intense situations.

Well-being is about *enjoying life*. If you don't enjoy climbing your tree, it isn't worth reaching the top. Successful self-discipline isn't about constantly nagging at yourself or being your own drill sergeant—it's about disconnecting when you clock out from your job. Put your life ahead of your job and you'll experience true joy.

If you find yourself needing some time to walk away from it all, use an **EBP** (Emergency Break Period). Give yourself five minutes to move around, do some deep breathing and pray. Make sure to please all five senses (sight, sound, smell, taste and touch) before getting back to the task at hand.

When it comes to execution, you can use small wins—accomplishing small goals—to give yourself momentum. That momentum can build confidence, which will help you establish resiliency and avoid making excuses.

The top motivator in execution is finding healthy competition—something or someone that will push you to greater heights. Once you have healthy competition in place, you'll use self-regulation to keep your emotions and thoughts in check. Like we talked about in our Execution Chapter, your ability to self-regulate will help you turn external factors in your favor.

For example, your boss will see that, even though you didn't get the promotion you were hoping for, you kept producing and working hard to hone your craft. The next time a promotion becomes available, it shall be yours!

As you work towards accomplishing your goals and executing your plan, there will be obstacles you'll need to overcome. That's where *perseverance* comes into play. Remember my story about accidentally deleting the book I was writing? *What's done is done.*

It isn't the failures or setbacks you experience that define you, it's how you *react* to those failures that determines who you are and whether or not you've established successful self-discipline. Instead of fearing failure and hoping it won't happen, embrace the fact that it *will* happen. Plan for how you'll react if a certain obstacle pops up. Find reassurance in the fact that, whenever you experience failure, you're one step closer to accomplishing your goal!

The climb to the top of your Self-Discipline Tree means nothing if you go about it the wrong way. Your reputation is the only thing that will remain when you retire, pass away, etc. What do you want to be remembered for? It's important to maintain strong *integrity* as you work to accomplish your dreams. Remember the *fruit of the Spirit*—love, joy, peace, patience, kindness, goodness, faithfulness, gentleness and self-control. You should keep an unwavering loyalty to these qualities. Some of them will come more naturally to you than others, and that's okay!

Self-discipline isn't about being perfect 100-percent of the time—no human achieves that. *Successful* self-discipline is about *remaining consistent* with your strengths while working to improve your weaknesses; it's a never-ending battle, but a fun and rewarding one nonetheless!

Lastly, you'll need strong and healthy accountability from yourself and others as you set out on this quest. No matter what goal you're trying to achieve, you'll accomplish a higher conversion rate on your goals if you self-assess and establish checkpoints for each of your goals; these will naturally create personal accountability that you can use to build *serious* momentum.

Then there's the matter of finding a strong support system that you can rely on. Think back to *The Inklings group* that C. S. Lewis and J. R. R. Tolkien were a part of. While all of those men shared different interests and passions, they pushed each other to speak their goals into existence by reading their poems and stories aloud.

Part of that support system is finding a strong *group* of mentors that can grant you reassurance, guidance, assistance and support. This will take time. Just stay open-minded and pick the brains of everyone you meet. As one of *my* mentors told me, "Accountability is the gauge of our degree of self-discipline." That goes for the support system that you build as well.

Throughout this book, we've used my Self-Discipline Tree as a metaphor for the different phases you'll experience on your way to attaining any goal, but you don't have to master all of these in one day. You might already be practicing a few phases in your life—others of them will take more time to develop. Use all of these stages—Vision, Goal-Setting, Organization, Cleansing, Exercise, Nutrition, Well-Being, Execution, Perseverance, Reputation and Accountability—to your benefit. Put the Self-Discipline Tree blueprint to the test in your life and I *promise* that you'll love the results.

The truth is, my friend, you've always had successful self-discipline within you. Now you have a concrete plan for how to summon it.

You've identified the goals you wish to accomplish. You have a blueprint for how you're going to reach the top of your Self-Discipline Tree. You even have a few ideas for how to embrace *and* overcome failure when—not if—they occur.

Now there's only one thing left to do: *Climb.*

Acknowledgments

Behind every great book is an army of people to thank. When I stop to think about all of the amazing and influential humans that helped make this book a possibility, I'm overwhelmed—in a good way. I've wanted to write a book ever since I was little, but it's no coincidence that this is happening now. God has blessed me with so many different mentors and friends, all of which contributed to this project in some form or fashion.

It all starts with my wife, Bre. You're constantly pushing me to become better and improve. You encouraged me when I went to write page one of this book, then encouraged me more when I accidentally deleted the book and had to write page one again. Somehow, you and I have taught each other to never stay stagnant in our personal or professional lives, and for that I'm grateful. You're not just my wife, you're my best friend!

Mom and Dad: you are the two biggest role models in my life. You've taught me that while life is filled with peaks and valleys, it's beautiful nonetheless. You two believed in me when no one else did. Even during the times I've made it easy to give up on me, you never have. You had to force feed self-discipline into my head, then wait years for any results to show. I'd like to think that's showing now, and it's all thanks to you!

Asher: even though you're only 8 months old at the moment, you've given me motivation and inspiration every day I went to work on this book. I hope this book has made you as proud of me as I am of you. Without you, I may have never worked up the courage to become an author.

Jennie and Justin: you both have made such a huge impression on my life. You are the biggest role models of mine outside of mom and dad, and you didn't disappoint. Your marriage is an inspiration to us all—whether you were working three jobs to make ends meet for your family or spotting me a $100 so I could provide groceries for mine. I can never repay you for the lessons you've taught Bre and I. You both are the true definition of perseverance and self-sacrifice.

Kim, Dylan, and Ty: we've been through so much together. Growing up with you three was a true blessing. All three of you work your tails off even at such a young age, and I couldn't be prouder. Each of you have unlimited potential, and I can't wait to see what trees you choose to climb!

Christian, Matt, Steven, Jake, and Jeff: you're all lifelong friends that encouraged me to never give up my creativity, imagination or personality—all three of which are poured out into this book. You helped me realize I had something to say, and a talent for writing that would allow me to say it.

George, Caryn, Alyssa, Mason and Kaylee: thank you for your support, but more importantly, thank you for welcoming me into your family. I'm honored to be a part of such a hard-working family. To George and Caryn specifically, thank you for raising such an amazing daughter.

To Pastor Dan Wegrzyn and Coach Bill Maddock: you both went on the journey of writing this book with me. Your verification and approval on this project were more valuable to me than you'll ever know.

To my editor and proof-reader, Chrissy Sokolowski: you helped me avoid *many* critical errors in creating this book. Offering your professional expertise for the flow and tone of this book meant the world to Bre and I.

To all those men and women that filled out my self-discipline surveys: your responses helped shaped the framework for this book. Heck, without you, there wouldn't even *be* a book. I treasure all of your friendships. This book is as equally yours as it is mine.

Carlton Irvis: you made me *look* like an author, even though I wasn't technically one just yet. Your photography career and my writing career are forever intertwined now, and I look forward to watching them both grow.

Pastor Joon Tavarez: those afternoons we spent in the coffee shop sparked the idea for this book. You're the one that challenged me to design a brand *beyond* the book. I owe you a great debt for that.

A very special thank you goes out to Jonathan Milligan, Mark Batterson, and Charles Duhigg: while we've never officially met, I consider all three of you to be my mentors, as well. Your books have had a huge influence on me. Not only did they shape this book, they've helped me shape my life and the way I view my career as a writer and author. One day, I hope you'll get the chance to read this book.

Lastly, I thank all of you that took the time to read this book. This being my first crack at writing one, I can only hope it gave you the solutions you deserve. There are many more books to come, and I can't wait for us to go on this journey together.

Notes

CHAPTER 1

1. "The meaning of life is to find your gift. The purpose of life is to give it away." (Picasso).

2. Belludi, Nagesh. *"To inspire, translate extrinsic motivation to intrinsic motivation."* Right Attitude, 8 Dec. 2015, https://www.rightattitudes.com/2015/12/08/translate-extrinsic-motivation-to-intrinsic-motivation/.

3. "Who wants to be a millionaire?." Wikipedia, https://en.wikipedia.org/wiki/Who_Wants_to_B e_a_ Millionaire%3F.

4. Rawes, Erika. "Top 5 money problems Americans face." USA Today, 20 Sept. 2020, https://www.usatoday.com/story/money/personalfinance/2014/09/20/wall-st-cheat-sheet-money-problems/15832929/.

5. Ramsey, Dave. "Dave Ramsey's 7 baby steps." Ramsey Solutions, https://www.ramseysolutions.com/dave-ramsey-7-baby-steps.

6. "Take the first step in faith. You don't have to see the whole staircase, just take the first step." (King)

7. Kenton, Will. "Strength, Weakness, Opportunity, and Threat (SWOT) analysis". Reviewed by Scott, Gordon.

Investopedia, 30 Mar. 2021, https://www.investopedia.com/terms/s/swot.asp.

8. Peele, Stanton. "What killed Anthony Bourdain?: Love addiction is worse the second time around." Reviewed by Ma, Lybi. Psychology Today, 7 Oct. 2018, https://www.psychologytoday.com/us/blog/addiction-in-society/201810/what-killed-anthony-bourdain.

9. "What is considered a good college GPA? surprising facts." University of the People, https://www.uopeople.edu/about/uopeople/.

CHAPTER 2

1. "Game cast between the St. Louis Rams and San Diego Chargers." Entertainment and Sports Programming Network, 30 Oct. 2006, https://www.espn.com/nfl/game?gameId=261029024.

2. Puskar, Gene J. "Read LaDainian Tomlinson's stirring Hall of Fame Speech: 'My story is America's story'." Time USA, 8 Aug. 2017, https://time.com/4891290/ladainian-tomlinson- pro-football-hall-of-fame-speech/.

3. "2000 TCU Horned Frogs football team." Wikipedia, https://en.wikipedia.org/wiki/2000_TCU_Horned_Frogs_football_team#Roster.

4. Evans, Sidney. "How to define your defining moments." Forbes, 3 Aug. 2017, https://www.forbes.com/sites/

forbescoachescouncil/2017/08/03/how-to-define-your-defining-moments/?sh=e8fc02e25d0f.

5. Curtin, Melanie. "In an 8-hour day, the average worker is productive for this many hours: It may make you feel better about leaving work early today." Inc, 21 July 2016, https://www.inc.com/melanie-curtin/in-an-8-hour-day-the-average-worker-is-productive-for-this-many-hours.html.

6. McKay, Dawn Rosenberg. "How to set short- and long-term career goals." The Balance Careers, 9 Dec. 2019, https://www.thebalancecareers.com/goal-setting-526182.

7. "The Harvard MBA Business School study on goal setting." Wanderlust Worker, https://www.wanderlustworker.com/the-harvard-mba-business-school-study-on-goal-setting/.

8. Mind Tools Content Team. "SMART goals: How to make your goals achievable." Mind Tools, https://www.mindtools.com/pages/article/smart-goals.htm.

9. Ryan, Chris. "What are the odds of high school football player reaching the NFL?" NJ.com, 8 Sep. 2015, https://www.nj.com/highschoolsports/article/what-are-the-odds-of-a-high-school-football-player-reaching-the-nfl.

CHAPTER 3

1. Lebowitz, Shana. "A sleep doctor says 4 types of animals represent how people sleep and these are the ideal daily routines for each." Business Insider, 29 Sept. 2016, https://

www.businessinsider.com/how-to-find-your-perfect-daily-routine-2016-9.

2. Becker, Joshua. "Top five regrets of the dying." Becoming Minimalist, https://www.becomingminimalist.com/top-five-regrets-of-the-dying/.

3. Coulson J.C., et al. "Exercising at work and self-reported work performance." International Journal of Workplace Health Management, vol. 1, no. 3, Sept. 2008, pp. 176-197. doi: 10.1108/17538350810926534.

4. Duhigg, Charles. The Power of Habit: Why We Do What We Do in Life and Business. New York, Random House, 7 Jan. 2014.

CHAPTER 4

1. "Being entirely honest with oneself is a good exercise." (Freud).

2. "Different types of relationships." Assert (B&H), https://assertbh.org.uk/wp-content/ uploads/2016/08/Different-Types-of-Relationships.pdf.

3. Anader, Lori. "Rumors, gossip, and your health." Reviewed by Ambardekar, Nayana. WebMD, 8 Feb. 2020, https://www.webmd.com/balance/health-rumors-gossip.

4. Hall, John. "12 easy ways to beat social media distraction effectively." Lifehack, 15 Feb. 2021, https://www.lifehack.org/885685/social-media-distraction.

5. Sweatt, Lydia. "15 inspiring quotes about never giving up." Success, 6 Apr. 2017, https://www.success.com/15-inspiring-quotes-about-never-giving-up/.

6. Scott, S.J. "Excellence is a habit: 7 lessons from this Aristotle quote." Develop Good Habits, 2019. https://www.developgoodhabits.com/excellence-habit/.

CHAPTER 5

1. Health, Heart. "80% of Americans don't get enough exercise and here's how much you actually need: New guidelines spell out how much physical activity to aim for." Cleveland Clinic, 20 Nov. 2018, https://health.clevelandclinic.org/80-of-americans-dont-get-enough-exercise-and-heres-how-much-you-actually-need/.

2. MacKay, Jory. "7 mental strategies for reaching your long term goals (at work and in life)." RescueTime, 3 Feb. 2021, https://blog.rescuetime.com/mental-strategies-long-term-goals/.

3. Duhigg, Charles. The Power of Habit: Why We Do What We Do in Life and Business. New York, Random House, 7 Jan. 2014.

4. Bryant, Kobe. The Mamba Mentality: How I Play. New York, MCD, 23 Oct. 2018.

CHAPTER 6

1. Healy, Ellen. "Weight loss and the 80% nutrition, 20% exercise rule." Genesis Health Clubs, 31 Aug. 2020, https://

www.genesishealthclubs.com/blog/nutrition/weight-loss-and-the-80-nutrition20-exercise-rule.html.

2. Brown, Harriet. "The weight of the evidence: It's time to stop telling fat people to become thin." Slate Group, 24 Mar. 2015, https://slate.com/technology/2015/03/diets-do-not-work-the-thin-evidence-that-losing-weight-makes-you-healthier.html.

3. Olien, Darin. SuperLife: The 5 Simple Fixes That Will Make You Healthy, Fit, and Eternally Awesome. New York, Harper Wave, 3 Jan. 2017.

4. Fetters, K. Aleisha. "How long does it really take to make healthy eating and exercise a habit?." U.S. News, 28 Apr. 2017, https://health.usnews.com/wellness/food/articles/2017- 04-28/how-long-does-it-really-take-to-make-healthy-eating-and-exercise-a-habit.

5. McLeod, Saul. "Pavlov's Dogs." Simply Psychology, 2018, https://www.simplypsychology.org/pavlov.html.

Chapter 7

1. "Ziggy Marley & The Melody Makers lyrics." AZ Lyrics, https://www.azlyrics.com/lyrics/ziggymarley/believeinyourselfarthurthemesong.html.

2. "To be a champ you have to believe in yourself when no one else will." (Robinson).

3. Duhigg, Charles. The Power of Habit: Why We Do What We Do in Life and Business. New York, Random House, 7 Jan. 2014.

4. Zach. "The optimal amount of time to spend working each day, according to research." Four Pillar Freedom, https://fourpillarfreedom.com/the-optimal-amount-of-time-to-spend- working-each-day-according-to-research/.

5. Raman, Ryan. "How to safely get vitamin d from sunlight." Healthline, 28 Apr. 2018, https://www.healthline.com/nutrition/vitamin-d-from-sun.

CHAPTER 8

1. Shpigel, Ben. How the Blues went from last place to the Stanley Cup finals. The New York Times, 22 May 2019, https://www.nytimes.com/2019/05/22/sports/st-louis-blues-stanley- cup-finals.html.

2. Jr, H. Jackson Brown. Life's Little Instruction Book: 511 Suggestions, Observations, and Reminders on How to Live a Happy and Rewarding Life. Nashville, Rutledge Hill, 1 Sept. 2000.

3. Wilson, Aaron. "Eighteen sacks for Rams' Robert Quinn." National Football Post, 23 Dec. 2013, https://www.nationalfootballpost.com/2008-2018-nfp-archive/latest-nfl-news/eighteen-sacks-for-rams-robert-quinn/.

Chapter 9

1. Moore, Meredith Leigh. "7 common obstacles to achieving your goals and how to get unstuck." Getting Untucked, 6 June 2018, https://www.gettingunstuckguide.com/post/trib e-methodology.

2. Legg, Timothy. "What is learned helplessness?" Medical News Today, https:/www.medicalnewstoday.com/articles/325355

3. Parren Alexandra. "Training: Research shows 43% of people expect to give up their new year's resolutions by February." Sundried, 12 Feb. 2021, https://www.sundried.com/blogs/training/research-shows-43-of-people-expect-to-give-up-their-new-years-resolutions-by-february.

4. Ahlin, Charlotte. "These books weren't appreciated when they first came out." Bustle, 3 May 2017, https://www.bustle.com/p/10-books-that-werent-appreciated-when-they-first-came-out-53224.

Chapter 10

1. Salm, Lauren. "70% of employers are snooping candidates' social media profiles." Career Builder, 15 June 2017, https://www.careerbuilder.com/advice/social-media-survey-2017.

2. The Holy Bible, New International Version. International Bible Society, Zondervan Corporation, 2001.

Chapter 11

1. Glyer, Diana. "C.S. Lewis, J. R. R. Tolkien, and the Inklings." C. S. Lewis, 16 April 2009, https://www.cslewis.com/c-s-lewis-j-r-r-tolkien-and-the-inklings/

2. "Find a job you enjoy doing, and you will never have to work a day in your life." (Twain)

3. "Father's Day: Inspirational father-son bond creates Olympic history." Olympics.com, 21 June 2020, https://olympics.com/tokyo-2020/en/news/fathers-day-inspirational-father-son-bond-creates-olympic-history

Conclusion

1. "Success". Oxford Languages. https://www.oxfordlearnersdictionaries.com/us/definition/american_english/success. 31 July 2021.

Made in United States
Orlando, FL
30 January 2023

29231236R00143